Irish Travellers

Sharon Bohn Gmelch
& George Gmelch

Irish Travellers

THE UNSETTLED LIFE

INDIANA UNIVERSITY PRESS   BLOOMINGTON • INDIANAPOLIS

This book is a publication of

Indiana University Press
Office of Scholarly Publishing
Herman B Wells Library 350
1320 East 10th Street
Bloomington, Indiana 47405 USA

iupress.indiana.edu

Telephone 800-842-6796
Fax 812-855-7931

∞ The paper used in this publication meets the minimum
requirements of the American National Standard for
Information Sciences—Permanence of Paper for Printed
Library Materials, ANSI Z39.48–1992.

Manufactured in China

Library of Congress Cataloging-in-Publication Data

Irish travellers : the unsettled life / Sharon Bohn Gmelch
and George Gmelch.
   pages cm
   ISBN 978-0-253-01453-5 (paperback)—
ISBN 978-0-253-01461-0 (ebook) 1. Irish Travellers
(Nomadic people) 2. Irish Travellers (Nomadic people)—
Pictorial works. 3. Irish Travellers (Nomadic people)—
Social conditions. 4. Ireland—Ethnic relations. I. Gmelch,
George. II. Title.
   DA927.4.T72G64 2014
   305.9'0691809415—dc23
                                      2014011875

1 2 3 4 5 19 18 17 16 15 14

To the Connors, Donoghue, and
Maughan families of Holylands
and their descendants

CONTENTS

Irish Travellers

1

FROM TINKERS TO TRAVELLERS

THE TRAVELLING PEOPLE HAVE, FOR GENERATIONS, STOOD ON THE BOTTOM rung of Ireland's social and economic ladder, a poor and stigmatized minority group. Until the 1960s most traveled through the countryside, at first on foot and later in horse-drawn carts and wagons, performing a variety of trades and services. Despite the value of the services they provided, they were regarded as inferior and regularly discriminated against, especially once they began migrating to urban areas in search of work. They were commonly called "tinkers" (from the trade of tinsmithing), "knackers" (from the practice of selling old horses for slaughter), and, beginning in the 1960s, "itinerants" (the less pejorative term introduced by government).

Although their lifestyle was and continues to be outwardly similar to that of English Gypsies or Roma, the Travelling People are native to Ireland. They are one of numerous indigenous nomadic groups—including the Swedish Resande, Norwegian Taters, Dutch Woonwagonbewoners, and Scottish Travellers—that have existed in Western Europe. Today approximately 29,000 Travellers live among a population of 4.5 million settled Irish, and they remain one of the least assimilated of Europe's itinerant groups.[1]

The early history of Ireland's Travelling People is obscure. Being illiterate, they left no written records of their own. As poor people living on the margin of settled society, they were largely ignored in Ireland's recorded history and literary works.[2] Genetic research conducted in the 1970s and an analysis of the DNA of forty individuals in 2010 clearly show,

John Ward fashions tins on the roadside outside Galway City in 1972.
Chimney sweeping equipment is tied to his bicycle.

however, that Travellers are native to Ireland and have lived there as long as anyone. Such research also conclusively shows that they are not Roma. Beyond that, only one thing is certain: not all Travelling families originated at the same time or in the same way. Some families' nomadism dates back centuries, while for others it is more recent. And many have genealogies mixed with both Travellers and settled people. Some undoubtedly began to travel as itinerant craftsmen and specialists because of the limited demand for their work in any one place. Others were originally peasants and laborers who voluntarily went on the road to look for work or else were forced onto it by eviction or for some personal reason—a problem with drink, the birth of an illegitimate child, or marriage to a "tinker."

Throughout Ireland's history a variety of occupational groups were nomadic. As early as the fifth century, metal workers or "whitesmiths" traveled the countryside fashioning jewelry, weapons, and horse trappings out of bronze, silver, and gold in exchange for food and lodging. Other specialists, including weavers, thatchers, musicians, and bards, also traveled Ireland's roads in past centuries. Ward, the Anglicized form of the Irish *Mac an Bhaird,* meaning "son of the bard," is one of the most common Traveller surnames, and the Wards are regarded by other Travellers as one of the oldest families on the road.[3]

In the twelfth century, "tinker" and "tynkere" appear in written records as trade or surnames for the first time. (The word "tinker" derives from the sound of the smith's hammer striking metal.) By the sixteenth century, itinerant tinkers were numerous enough in Ireland and Scotland to give newly arriving Roma stiff competition. Tinkers are specifically mentioned in the numerous statutes enacted from the sixteenth to the nineteenth century in the British Isles against vagrancy and begging. By 1835, when Britain's Poor Inquiry Commissioners visited Ireland—then a British colony—to collect evidence on the state of the poor, local people differentiated tinkers from other people then living on the road. A resident of county Mayo reported, "The wives and families accompany the tinker while he strolls about in search of work, and always beg. They intermarry with one another, and form a distinct class." A resident of Donegal similarly stated that they were "the only class of beggars whose habits of mendicancy become hereditary; the other vagrants beg through . . . [temporary] want of employment."[4] Yet another respondent described three generations traveling the roads together, which, at the very minimum, meant that they had been itinerant since the late 1700s.

At the outbreak of World War II, Ireland's Travellers were still a nomadic and rural people. Their most common occupations, besides making tinware, were cleaning chimneys, dealing in donkeys and horses, peddling small household wares, and picking crops, all in exchange for food, clothing, and cash. While many Travellers had a primary trade, they were also opportunistic. As one man we knew astutely stated, "The tinker was a man who thought of a hundred ways of surviving. If he was selling delph [crockery] and the delph failed him, he'd switch to something else. Maybe he'd buy something else or resell it. There were always a hundred ways out. This was the real tinker, not the tinsmith. He was a better survivor than the rest." Travellers also made clothespins, brooms, and baskets; repaired umbrellas; sharpened knives; collected and recycled horse hair, feathers, and bottles; and exploited the superstitions and hopes of the settled population through begging, fortune telling, and bogus money-making schemes. They were truly jacks of all trades.

Most families traveled and camped on the roadside from St. Patrick's Day in mid-March (when, it was said, the stones turned over in the water and the cold went out of the winter)

Mother and children line up for a photograph in front of their
shelter tents on the northern outskirts of Dublin, 1975.

until November, when wet, bone-chilling weather returned. Some then moved into modest cottages in what they considered to be their home village, while others took shelter in
abandoned "waste" houses in the countryside. While traveling, families seldom remained
in one place for more than a couple of weeks, staying only as long as work was available.
Most families traveled regular circuits through two or three neighboring counties and were
well known to local people, even acquiring affectionate nicknames like Bawling Moll. But
some families traveled widely and had weaker ties to the settled population. And although
Travellers were valued for the services they performed and for the news and stories they
carried, most country people were also glad to see them go. Nomads are usually regarded
with a degree of suspicion by sedentary populations, no matter how mutually beneficial
their relationship.

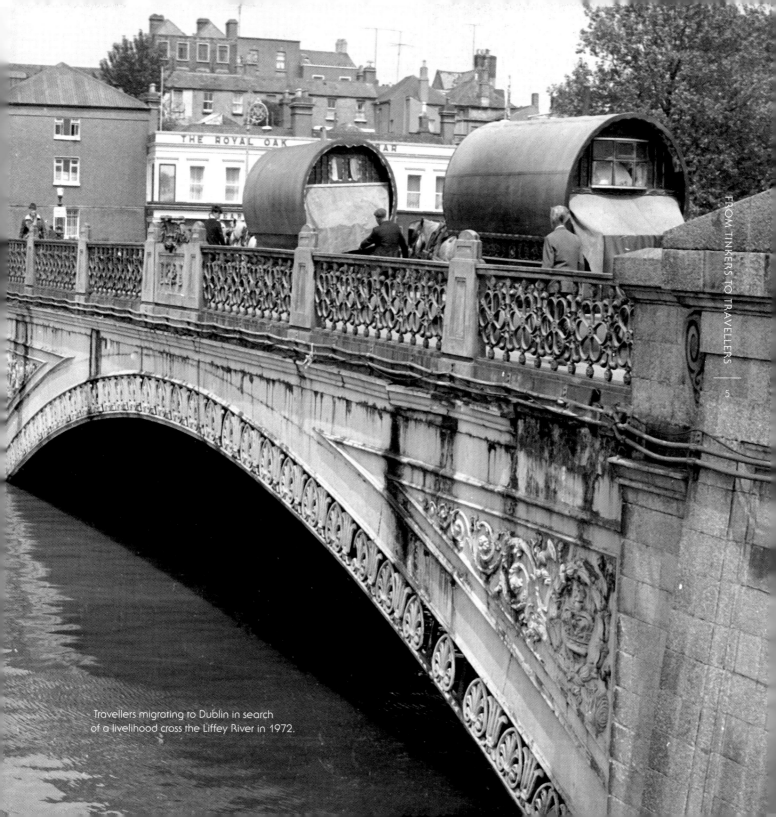

Travellers migrating to Dublin in search
of a livelihood cross the Liffey River in 1972.

As Ireland developed following World War II, the rural economy of Travellers changed dramatically. Plastic containers and the availability of cheap mass-produced tin and enamelware eliminated the tinsmith's work. Other trades and services also rapidly became obsolete. With the introduction of tractors and farm machinery like the beet digger, the demand for the horses some Travellers dealt in and the need for seasonal agricultural laborers disappeared. As rural bus service expanded and more country people could afford cars, shopping in town became easier, and people no longer needed the small goods that Travelling women once brought to their doors. Some Travellers moved to England at this time to work on construction sites or to collect scrap metal. Most, however, migrated to large provincial towns and cities within Ireland like Dublin, Limerick, and Cork in order to find work and sign on to the "dole."

There they camped on any open land they could find: roadside verges, fields, and derelict building sites in the city center. Most Travelling men turned to collecting scrap metal from homeowners and construction sites, separating it by metal type and selling it by weight to metal merchants and foundries. Some salvaged cars, selling parts directly from their roadside camps. Meanwhile, Travelling women with a baby and at least one young child in tow pushed their prams from door to door in the suburbs asking housewives for "a bit of help" in a modified version of rural peddling. Some women and teenage girls begged on city streets.

Largely in response to this migration—which created problems for urban residents and starkly highlighted the poverty under which most Travellers lived—a national volunteer movement emerged to deal with what became known as the "itinerant problem." Its goal was to settle Travelling families on "sites" where they would have basic services (for example, electricity, running water, toilets) and from which their children could attend school. Although some attention was given to providing for families who wished to remain nomadic, the hope was that Travellers would eventually move into houses and assimilate into mainstream Irish society. The logo of the "settlement movement" was a winding road leading to a house. It was in the early days of this dramatic change, in 1971, that we moved into a camp on the outskirts of Dublin to begin our first research among the Travellers.

LIVING WITH IRISH TRAVELLERS

In the jargon of anthropology, we would be doing "fieldwork" based largely on "participant observation." It was a rewarding and at times challenging initiation into Traveller life—and personally maturing as well. We were young Americans from comfortable middle-class suburban homes, a radically different background from the hand-to-mouth nomadic existence most Irish Travellers then lived. Although we spoke the same language, at times it hardly seemed so, so different were our life experiences. We were graduate students working toward our PhDs, while few Travellers could read or write. We came from small families—George's was considered fairly large at four children and mine typical at two—while Travellers had some of the largest in the Western world. The three oldest women in camp had each given birth more than twenty times, although not all infants had survived. This fact suggested another difference between us, which could also be read on most people's deeply lined faces, namely the hardship of their lives. Most Travellers at the time lacked the basic amenities and services that we and settled Irish people took for granted, like running water, toilets, and medical and dental care. Women's lives were especially arduous, as they bore the brunt of feeding, clothing, cleaning, and minding their many children.

When we returned to Ireland in 2011 much had changed. In 1973, a year after we left the field, Ireland joined the European Economic Community (EEC), which boosted the country's economy and over the next several decades introduced a host of new perspectives and policies that radically transformed the nation. But the most significant change that had taken place was that Travellers in Ireland were no longer nomads. Today the vast majority live in houses; others live stationary lives in caravans (trailers) on official sites. How has settlement changed Travellers' lives and their understanding of who they are? How do different generations of Travellers make sense of it all? Armed with several hundred photographs that George had taken during our early fieldwork, we returned to Ireland to explore such questions.

THE IMPORTANCE OF PHOTOGRAPHS

Although most people find photographs intrinsically interesting, they have special significance for Travellers. They are valued not only for the personal memories they evoke and as family mementos but also as "evidence" of a former way of life and their history as a people. This is true even for photographs taken as recently as ours. Travellers in the 1970s had virtually no written history or literature of their own. Fortunately, this is no longer the case. Today everything from social science studies, journalistic accounts, and government reports to novels, personal memoirs written by Travellers, and videos posted on YouTube document their lives. This is a positive development and means that future generations of Travellers and historians will have a rich trove of material to work with. But this does not change the fact that many pages of prior Traveller history are virtually blank. Photographs fill some of the void. And for many Travellers whose literacy is still limited, photographs remain more accessible than text.

Photography is a powerful medium. Recognizing its capacity to evoke emotion and to reveal rather than merely tell, we published in 1976, together with *Irish Times* photographer

A quiet roadside camp in county Cork in 1972. This family still has horse-drawn barrel-top wagons, although the transition to motorized transport is also evident.

Pat Langan, a photographic book about Travellers.[5] We hoped then that the positive and non-stereotypical glimpse it provided of Travellers' everyday lives might reduce the prejudice that existed against them. We also knew that photographs would make the book appealing and accessible to Travellers. The book proved popular, received significant media attention, and to our surprise it won the Irish Book Publishers' Book of the Year award. To what extent it softened public attitudes toward Travellers, especially in the long term, is impossible to judge.

In 2001 I returned to Ireland for research and showed some of George's photographs—black-and-white prints and color slides—to several groups of Travellers. One was a small and rather subdued mix of middle-aged and older women at Exchange House, a Dublin organization providing addiction, education, and youth services to Travellers. After chatting over biscuits and tea, the women sat back to watch the slide show I'd prepared. Murmuring to one another as the images flashed on the screen, their uniform reaction was nostalgia for life on the road, its open air, and "freedom," despite the hardship.

Several weeks later, I showed the same slides and some black-and-white prints to two families we had lived with during our fieldwork. Adults laughed at their appearance thirty years earlier and stood up frequently to point out relatives on the screen to their children. Some images showed Travellers in other parts of the country living in "bender" and "shelter" tents. The children and grandchildren had never seen such tents before and knew little of this former, yet comparatively recent, way of life. When the lights came back on, one twenty-year-old sat silently on the living room sofa, surrounded by animated cousins and siblings, with a furrowed brow and pensive expression. When I asked what he thought of the slides, he finally muttered, "Embarrassed." He was ashamed to see his family's and other Travellers' past poverty so evident in images of dirty faces and tattered clothes and tents, wagons, and battered trailers parked amid piles of scrap metal and scattered debris. His reaction in particular made me think about the possibility of returning someday with additional photographs to more systematically elicit Travellers' thoughts about their changing lives.

Ten years later, in 2011, we were finally ready to do so. Our decision to return was reinforced when we learned of Travellers' reactions to an exhibition of George's photographs at a South County Dublin library. To the surprise of its organizers, enthusiastic crowds of Travelling People, most of whom had never before stepped foot in a library, arrived. Librarian Breda Bollard described the scene to us in an e-mail: "When the exhibition arrived we had a young Traveller girl here, and she helped me choose which photographs to display. We

A tent made from grain bags, plastic, and canvas provides shelter for a
Travelling family in the Midlands, 1972. Note the handmade button-covered purse
known as a "pocket" carried by the young woman (identified as Mary Mongan).

picked a few to put into the local community magazine *The Wag Mag*. When the magazine
was delivered to the Traveller sites in the area, the response was immediate. . . . Extended
families contacted their extended families, and they traveled here from all parts of Ireland
and one couple from England." They were often "anxious to tell us their stories," she went
on. "Often these were the only images available on those who had died—often tragically.
There were heartbreaking scenes, with grown men fighting back tears at seeing pictures of
long dead relatives. Great elation at finding photographs of relatives now scattered." Many
of the Travellers who came wanted prints to take away, which the library provided. We later
saw several of these prominently displayed in Traveller homes. Some had been profession-
ally enlarged and printed on canvas. The librarians also reported some tension, with a few
Travellers asking them not to provide copies of certain images to particular people because
of family feuds. Clearly, George's photographs from the 1970s had great meaning to the
families portrayed in them.

What follows is the story of our return to Ireland that summer and of what Travellers—and some of the settled people who have worked closely with them—told us about how their lives have changed. George took new photographs, too, to help document these changes. What appears here, though, is not an exhaustive account of these changes; we use statistics and new scholarship on Travellers sparingly. Instead, it recounts a more personal and selective journey, one that focuses on the topics Travellers raised during our conversations—prompted both by photographs and questions—and on our own comparisons of what their lives are like today with what they had been in the early 1970s, when we lived among them. Since this is primarily their story, we have included the personal narratives of five individuals, which more evocatively convey than we could many of the nuances of the transformation that has taken place in Travelling life.

Finding and revisiting families we had lived with forty years earlier was a profoundly rewarding experience, as was meeting new families. There was also sadness. Many of the people we had lived with, including all of the adult men, have since died, and so have a startling number of younger people—a stark reminder of the hardship of Travelling life. Today, fewer than 3 percent of Travellers live to age sixty-five, compared to 11 percent of the general Irish population. Fortunately, many people we knew remain. Most were children during our fieldwork but now have children and grandchildren of their own. It was gratifying to discover that we had become part of the history and folklore of these families.[6] For us, living with Irish Travellers will always be one of the most profound experiences of our lives.

2

FIRST FIELDWORK

IT WAS THE SUMMER OF 1970 AND MY FIRST TIME IN IRELAND. I HAD COME to participate in an anthropology field school and been placed in a small fishing and farming community in county Kerry.[1] It was on the drive there that I first became aware of Irish Travellers, who were camped on the roadside in barrel-top wagons. I was intrigued, but it was George who had the first opportunity to work with them. He arrived in Ireland in mid-July and while waiting in Dublin for my program to end was offered work by physical anthropologist Michael Crawford, who was studying Traveller genetics.[2] George collected demographic information on the families in Crawford's study and, on the side, took some photographs.

Before leaving Ireland we bought a copy of *The Report of the Commission on Itinerancy,* the only publication we could find on Travellers. Published seven years earlier, it documented their poverty, illiteracy, and short life spans as well as the problems their nomadism was creating for the house-dwelling population, especially in Irish cities. Back in graduate school at the University of California at Santa Barbara that fall, we told a faculty advisor, Charles Erasmus, about Travellers and showed him some of George's photographs. He was fascinated and surprised to learn that no anthropologist had previously studied them. He urged us to abandon our plans of going to Mexico for our doctoral research and to pursue funding for Ireland instead. His enthusiasm was infectious. The dream of most anthropologists at the time, although rarely achievable, was to find a culture that had not been previously studied. Soon we were reading everything we could on Ireland and on nomadic groups similar to Travellers world-wide to start formulating research questions. I wanted to understand how Travellers who are so fundamentally like other Irish people—English-speaking, Roman Catholic, and indigenous to the country—had maintained a separate identity for generations. George was interested in their cityward migration and how they were adapting to urban life. Convinced that these were two of the most significant issues to examine and with modest research grants to support us, we set off for Ireland in the summer of 1971 immediately after passing our "comps."

At home in Santa Barbara, California, a few days before we left for Ireland in 1971.

Our Aer Lingus flight landed in Dublin on July 19, and our fieldwork began on the cab ride into the city when George asked the driver about Travellers. "The government is trying to house them," he explained, "but they don't want to be locked up." In what proved to be a common stereotype at the time, he added, "One family got a house, but they let the horses inside and cut the banisters up for firewood." He claimed to have seen a horse looking out their second-story window.

After checking into a bed and breakfast and catching a few hours' sleep, we made a list of things we needed to do: rent a flat, buy a used car, obtain a year's visa, and contact local officials about our research. Eager to get underway, George phoned Eithne Russell, a social worker he'd met the previous summer who worked with Travellers. She was attending a Traveller wedding the next day and invited us along, assuring us that the family wouldn't

Mags Maughan and Jim Connors's wedding in Dublin, 1971.

mind. In fact, she thought they'd be delighted to have some Americans there. As it turned out, George had met some of the Connors family the summer before and had mailed photographs back to them, so we were welcome.

The ceremony for the arranged marriage between Jim Connors and Mags Maughan took place at the Church of the Good Shepherd in Churchtown, a nearby suburb. I expected a large, gregarious crowd, but only a couple dozen people were there, and an air of detachment pervaded the gathering. Most of the men stood outside the church, while the bride's father and female relatives shifted uncomfortably on the pews inside. The fifteen-year-old bride

seemed shy and looked somewhat woebegone in her wrinkled and ill-fitting wedding dress. The groom's expression was more difficult to decipher. When the priest arrived, he took the couple by their elbows and jockeyed them into position in front of the altar. Perhaps unnecessarily, I felt embarrassed for them as he instructed them, in what seemed to me an unnecessarily loud and impatient tone, on what to say and when to say it. A handful of neighborhood children drifted in during the ceremony and stood at the back, gawking at the spectacle before them. And suddenly it was over, the customary Mass omitted. As the couple emerged from the church, a young *garda* (police officer) leaned out his patrol car window and called Jim over, advising him to "start out right" and be "well-behaved." We learned from Eithne later that Jim was out of jail on bail for the ceremony and that petty larceny was a growing problem among Travellers in the city. We left soon after, heads spinning from this glimpse of what was to come.

Within a week we had purchased a ten-year-old VW Beetle, leased a small "bedsitter" or studio apartment, and begun visiting Traveller encampments around the city. One of the first issues we faced as fledgling anthropologists was delineating the boundaries of the population we hoped to study. As graduate students participating in field schools

The *tigíns* of Labre Park, Ireland's first Traveller site, located in Ballyfermot on the west side of Dublin, 1971.

in Mexico and Ireland, we had lived in small villages. Dublin, on the other hand, was a large city with 1,500 Travellers scattered around in fifty camps. Some were temporary roadside encampments of two or three families; others were larger groupings of up to a dozen families, which had sprung up in open fields. The government had also established three official sites for as many as forty families. As lone researchers planning to do in-depth participant observation research, we needed to find a "community" where we could live with Travellers.

After visiting most of the camps around the city, we began concentrating on two official sites. Both had large, somewhat stable populations. Labre Park, located in Ballyfermot on the west side of Dublin, was the first government site built for Travellers. It then housed thirty-nine families in a long row of small one-room dwellings called *tigíns,* with extra family members spilling over into caravans and wagons parked nearby. Holylands was an undeveloped site located in Churchtown on the southern edge of the city. It was little more than a tree-ringed field with two strips of blacktop on which families parked their wagons and trailers. A single water tap, a rarely used outhouse, and a small "watchman's hut" manned during the day by a city employee were the only amenities for twenty families.

Upon arriving in a camp, we'd park our battered VW and walk off in separate directions to approach individuals or groups of Travellers and attempt to engage them in conversation. Our first impressions were not particularly flattering and undoubtedly colored by our own insecurity. The men looked tough and intimidating with their weather-beaten faces, dark tobacco-stained fingers, and evasive manner. The women, although less forbidding because many were pregnant and somewhat matronly, also seemed distant. Fieldwork among Travellers, we feared, might be more difficult than we expected.

Travellers' reactions to us varied. On early visits we were usually surrounded by children clamoring for handouts—"Ah, miss, could you give us a few coppers?"—as they did from most "buffers" or non-Travellers they met. We never gave since this would have cast us in a role that was incompatible with fieldwork and the friendships we hoped to create. No matter which site or camp we visited during those first weeks, the men remained aloof. Sometimes George would go up to a group of men standing around a campfire only to have it disintegrate as they drifted away, one by one, until eventually he was alone. It was difficult not to take such rebuffs personally. I had more luck with the women, but even they were not always that approachable. Some people were curious about us; others suspicious. We didn't fit into any familiar category: social worker, journalist, settlement committee volunteer, government official, clergy, or police. On top of that, we were Americans.

Fieldwork, especially the early stages, is a lot like childhood. You're untutored in the culture and the nuances of language, unsure of what behavior is appropriate, and forced to learn largely by trial and error. Moreover, you're dependent on the cooperation of people you hardly know. I was always on guard during the early weeks, consciously monitoring my behavior, trying to act appropriately: wanting to be friendly but not too friendly, wanting to show interest without appearing overly curious or intrusive. I ate whatever food was offered me, casually negotiated my way around scrap piles and animal excreta, and strived to act composed no matter what happened, which included sitting on mattresses saturated with baby urine on a couple occasions.

Travellers often asked me the same questions, even during the course of a single conversation: "Are you married? Is he your husband? How long have you been married? Do you have children? Don't you like children? Are you from America? Have you seen cowboys? Do you know Elvis?" We had few common experiences on which to base more wide-ranging

Biddy Doran Connors and "Old Jim" Connors, the heads
of the Connors "clan," at Holylands, 1971.

A typical morning at Holylands in 1971 as men and older boys head out to collect scrap metal, passing our car and campsite.

conversations. I also came to view their questions as a test of my consistency and truthfulness. Some days the thought of seeking out people to talk to, risking rejection, answering the same questions, and giving the same explanations over and over was almost too much to bear.

At first most of our conversations were with children, teenagers, and the elderly. We tried to clarify our role as American university students who wanted to learn what it was like to be a Traveller. We explained about writing doctoral dissertations, which they interpreted to mean books. When they asked how long we were going to stay and we answered "a year," they were skeptical. After repeated visits, however, people began to realize that we might be serious. As we became more familiar, Travellers became friendlier. Gradually we were developing rapport. Not being Irish may have worked to our advantage, lessening suspicions that we were something other than what we claimed.

After several weeks spent commuting between camps, we chose Holylands as our primary research site. The layout of the camp was better than Labre Park for fieldwork since families were camped in wagons and caravans facing one another across a central field rather than strung out single-file. This made daily life readily observable. Holylands also had a better cross-section of the Travelling community. Some families hailed from the more prosperous East and the Midlands, while others were from the poorer West. Some had been living in the city for nearly a decade, while others were recent arrivals and still quite mobile. Besides the stable core of families who remained on the site the entire year of our research, another dozen or so families came and went. But above all, more families at Holylands than at Labre Park had been overtly receptive to our visits.

Although we had met most of the families living at Holylands by the end of the first month and felt quite comfortable with them, commuting to the camp each day from our bedsitter was proving unsatisfactory. Travellers did not have fixed daily routines, and most made plans on the spur of the moment. Some days we would arrive in camp to find virtually everyone gone or else learn that the person one of us had most hoped to speak with was away for the day, had returned to the road, or had gone to England. George's attempts to arrange to accompany various men scrap collecting or to go on horse-buying trips were no more successful. He might arrive at the site at 9:30 AM and then wait for hours, never certain they wouldn't decide to skip the activity altogether. Understandably, our appointments were far more important to us than to them.

Increasingly, we felt that we were missing out on important events. This fear was reinforced each time we arrived in camp to be told something like, "You should have been here last night; the guards [police] came up and took Big John." Most important, we wanted to lose our outsider status and get "backstage," to use sociologist Erving Goffman's metaphor, to blend into the background of camp life so that people would feel comfortable and act naturally around us. Travellers were used to dealing with non-Travellers in superficial and manipulative ways. Begging and door-to-door dealing, for example, required them to be skilled at impression management. It was important for us to view their lives from the inside, to observe everyday behavior and try to learn what Travellers really thought. Moreover, because Travellers had never been studied in-depth before, we felt a need to collect as wide

An inebriated Nan Collins Maughan jokes with Mim Connors in front of
our wagon while young Mylee Connors looks on, 1971.

a range of ethnographic information as possible. Only living in a camp would enable us to do this.

Early in the second month of our fieldwork, several people suggested that we buy a wagon and move to the site. They said it was foolish for us to be paying rent when we could be living at Holylands for free. One day Red Mick Connors and Mick Donoghue took George around to other camps in the city looking for a good barrel-top wagon to buy, and within a week they found one for 100 pounds (250 USD). It was in need of paint and a few repairs, but this gave us something tangible to do each day when we arrived in camp. And now that it was clear we planned to move in, the social distance between ourselves and Travellers lessened.

As we worked on our wagon, people stopped by to give advice, lend a hand, or simply chat. Some days we arrived in camp to discover that someone had worked on our wagon in our absence. Michael Donoghue painted its undercarriage and wheels a bright canary yellow—their proper color. His father, Mick, made a new window frame for the broken one in our front door. Paddy Maughan found replacement shafts for the wagon and later helped George bargain for a horse, a large black mare named Franny. When our fieldwork was over, we sold her back to Paddy at the same price, not realizing she was in foal and, therefore, worth considerably more. I made curtains for the wagon's windows and laid red linoleum tiles on its tiny floor. Nanny Nevin gave me a lucky horseshoe to nail above the door. Once the repairs were complete, we bought some camping gear—sleeping bags, lantern, pots and pans, and a small camp stove—and moved in.

Our transition from regular visitors to residents was completed the first night when we were awakened around midnight by the roar of lorries and vans racing into camp, followed by loud talking and laughter as people returned home from the pubs. Not long after the camp had settled down to sleep, a loud argument broke out in the caravan next to us. Accusations and obscenities were exchanged, followed by screams, thuds, and shattering glass. I crept out of bed and cautiously peeked through the front window, catching an oblique glimpse of my neighbor as she staggered out her door. A shiver of fear swept over me as I wondered what would happen next, but soon everything quieted down again and the camp returned to sleep.

The next morning we acted as if nothing had happened. Everyone we saw, however, seemed subdued and somewhat sheepish. When Nanny Nevin walked by our wagon, she coyly asked how well we'd slept but made no direct reference to the fight. Sam, the eight-year-old son of the family involved, came closest when he said to me later, "You must have

Conversations around the campfire were an important part of fieldwork.
Here Sharon sits with Sally, Nan, and Mick Donoghue and other camp members, 1972.

learned a lot last night." Indeed we had. Many of the polite public fictions maintained for visiting outsiders had been broken. We soon discovered that Thursdays, the day that men collected the "dole" or unemployment payment, were days of heavy drinking for many, often followed by arguments and, not infrequently, by domestic violence after they returned home.

Living on the site dramatically improved our rapport. We could now talk to people casually while going about our daily chores of hauling water, preparing meals, or searching for our mare. We no longer had to force conversations as the visitor must but could wait for opportunities to talk to arise naturally. People became accustomed to us and seemed comfortable with our presence. We had gotten backstage and were beginning to know and share the private lives of Travellers.

Our research and life soon fell into an enjoyable routine. Because Travellers spent much of their time out of doors, they were more accessible than people had been in villages in the west of Ireland and Mexico. Every family lit a campfire in the morning and kept it going until they went to bed at night. A blackened kettle of water was kept hot, and pots of tea were brewed throughout the day. Much of our fieldwork involved talking to people while sitting around a campfire. At night most men and some younger couples went off to the pubs to drink. For several weeks we wanted to join them, since we imagined it would be a good place to talk, but didn't feel confident enough to ask. Then one evening we were invited along by some of the Connors men and learned that they had been talking about doing so for a while but hadn't been sure that we would want to be seen with them in public or go to the few working-class pubs that served Travellers. After that, we joined them many evenings, often sitting around the campfire afterward to talk and drink some more.

Pa Maughan and James Browne play cricket as John Maughan looks on, 1972.

Sports provided another outlet for socializing. The boys and younger men in camp often played handball or a version of cricket using a tennis ball and a board as a bat. George had discovered the value of sports in developing rapport and creating friendships two years earlier while living in Mexico after he joined a village basketball team. With this experience in mind, and seeking a way to get more exercise, he suggested to several men that they organize a soccer team. No one at Holylands had played on an organized team before, but the idea quickly spread, and soon a team was formed and christened the "Wagon Wheels." During the week the teenagers and younger men practiced on a nearby school pitch, often having to clear it first of their horses, which they illegally grazed there. On weekends they drove to different venues around the city to compete. Their matches—all against teams comprising non-Travellers—were eagerly anticipated and underwent endless analysis afterward. George's role in organizing the team and his play as goalie further cemented our place in camp.

Most of our data were collected through participant observation, that is, by observing and participating in the everyday life of the camp and then writing up detailed field notes. Participation, however, is always a matter of degree. We didn't, for example, regularly accompany Travellers on their daily economic rounds. Our time was usually better spent staying in camp where we could have extended conversations with people, observe the ebb and flow of camp life, and be around when unexpected events occurred. We also used the hours when most adults were away on their economic rounds to pursue other aspects of our research such as visiting archives and government offices, interviewing settled people who worked with Travellers, or typing up our field notes.[3]

Still, it was important to directly experience what men and women did when they left camp each day to earn a living and to observe the kinds of interactions they had with settled people. On a few occasions I accompanied women on their suburban begging rounds. Although I did not pretend to be a Traveller by altering my clothes or donning a shawl, as several women suggested, I did go up to doors on my own, simply explaining to the surprised householders who answered my knock that I was an American student who knew the people I was with and that they were genuinely needy. I was given the same items Travelling women were given: flour, sugar, butter, tins of peas, used clothing. Similarly, George occasionally accompanied Travelling men on their scavenging and scrap metal–collecting rounds, although they made it clear to him that a "scholar" like himself, by which they meant an educated person, should not knock on any doors.

Our mare, Franny, rests while Anthony Maughan, Michael Donoghue, and Sharon eat lunch on the way to Blessington, county Wicklow, 1972.

Being with Travellers in public was often insightful. Once we went with Mick Donoghue on his scrap-collecting and knife-sharpening rounds and directly encountered the disrespect Travellers often faced. As we drove through a middle-class neighborhood in Mick's horse-drawn cart, several youths ran after us yelling, "Knacker," pretending they were going to jump onto the back of the cart. On another occasion we joined Bun Connors on a horse-buying trip to the Midlands, memorable largely for what it revealed about the limitations of illiteracy. Bun followed a convoluted route in his lorry, passing up several road signs that clearly indicated a more direct way. We also hitched our mare, Franny, to our barrel-top wagon and took a trip into the Wicklow countryside for several days with the help of teenagers Anthony Maughan and Michael Donoghue in order to learn firsthand

Sons from the three "clans" at Holylands—the Maughans, Connorses, and Donoghues—climb on a derelict truck, 1971.

what traveling entailed. We also experienced some of the discrimination Travellers faced when, soon after making camp the first day, a farmer rode by on his bicycle and not long after a *garda* arrived: the farmer had accused us of chopping his fence posts for firewood and breaking a window in one of his outbuildings.

Much of our data were gathered through conversation or informal interviews with Travellers. Every morning we each jotted down the topics or questions we hoped to explore during the day and, when conversations lagged, steered conversations toward them. In the process we learned when (and when not) to ask direct questions as well as what subjects were acceptable to broach in front of whom. Early weeks at Holylands were spent learning about the logistics of traveling, the skills of tinsmithing and rural peddling, what settled people were like in different parts of the country, and family stories and backgrounds. As time passed, we left the historical and general behind and raised contemporary and potentially sensitive issues—welfare, discrimination in the city, drinking, family problems, and trouble with the law. We kept separate field notes and regularly reviewed them to see what information was thin or missing, formulating new questions to ask. When we had heard the same answers often enough to be confident of the accuracy of the information, we moved on to new topics.

We seldom took notes openly. Since most Travellers were illiterate and would not have known what we were writing, we felt it would be insensitive to do so. Only when the information we were being told was detailed (for example, involving many names, using Gammon vocabulary) did we openly take notes.[4] Instead, we returned to our wagon at the earliest opportunity and jotted down key words, phrases, and details that we could later flesh out and type up as complete field notes.

Although we each arrived in Ireland with a clear "problem" to study, anthropologists of our day were less concerned with theory than with ethnography—detailed descriptions of a culture. Furthermore, no one at the time had done extended fieldwork with Travellers, and little was known about their lives. One Irish sociology student, Patricia McCarthy, had lived with Travellers in Galway for a month and written a master's thesis applying Oscar Lewis's culture of poverty model to them, but nothing more had been written.[5] We believed we should collect as much data about their culture and history as possible, whether or not we could see a direct connection to either of our specific projects. George, for example, collected data on and later wrote an article for a folklore journal about the history of the Travellers' barrel-top wagons.

Many topics came up spontaneously, initiated by Travellers. Individuals frequently stepped up into our wagon, shut the door, and sat down to talk. Anthropologists as neutral outsiders who have shown great interest in the people they live among often become confidants. Information and feelings that could not be shared with other Travellers because of family rivalries or fear that the information would be used against them later could be discussed with us. George and I didn't need to remind each other never to reveal to other Travellers what we learned in private.

Like all anthropologists, we relied heavily upon the friendship and assistance of a few individuals who became our primary teachers or "key informants," in the jargon of the time. At Holylands, we were fortunate to develop friendships and collaborations with members of each of the three major "clans" (the word Travellers used for their large extended family

Nan Donoghue, 1972.

groupings) living in camp: the Connorses, Donoghues, and Maughans. One of these was Nan Donoghue, the woman who had been beaten our first night in camp and whose life story I later wrote and published.

Fieldwork is a process of adjustment for both anthropologists and the people they study. We had habits Travellers regarded as unusual, if not bizarre. Children at first gathered around us in the morning to watch us brush our teeth, talking and pointing: "Ah, would you look, Sharon's scrubbing her teeth." They were surprised that I knew how to drive a car and that I wore slacks or jeans, something almost no Travelling women did at the time. They found it odd when one of us went for a walk alone, as they did nearly everything in the company of others. Even reading a book was unusual since all but one Holylander were illiterate. When some women asked me why we did not have children, I told them about birth control pills. Others remarked with mild amazement that George and I never yelled at each other. (We probably did, but not in their company.)

Our most difficult adjustment was to the loss of privacy. Wagon walls were thin, and there were always people around. For Travellers, the idea that anyone would want to be on their own was alien. They had large families and lived in crowded conditions. Travellers, especially youths and men, routinely entered other families' dwellings without warning or sat down at another family's campfire to listen for a while and then leave, sometimes without uttering a word. We could expect visitors at any time. George installed a latch inside our wagon's Dutch-style front doors as a deterrent, but most people merely opened the top windows and leaned in to talk or else reached down, unhooked the latch, and entered. This loss of privacy was a small price to pay for the acceptance and friendship we received as well as the data it provided.

While we made an effort to get to know everyone at Holylands, it was inevitable that we would rely upon some individuals and families more than on others. We had little contact with one of the Maughan families, primarily because the adults drank heavily and were often difficult, creating problems for everyone in camp. The eldest son, "Big John," age twenty-six, was sometimes abusive. At various times he tossed a burning log under our car, threw a rock through our wagon window, and challenged George to a fight. George described one incident in his field notes:

> Yesterday as we were driving out of the site, Big John stepped in front of the car. He was drunk and wanted a ride downtown. We reluctantly made room for him. A couple miles down the road, he changed

his mind and insisted we take him back to camp. Already irritated and not wanting to appear weak, I told him politely yet firmly that he could either get out of the car now or continue on with us. He refused, so I pulled into a police station which happened to be nearby. As soon as I stopped, he jumped out of the car and we drove off. This morning he came up to the fire where I was sitting with Red Mick, Jim and Mylee. He was drunk again and announced that he had been in jail all night because of me. Waving his fist, he said, "I'm giving you fifteen minutes to pull your wagon out of this camp or I'll burn you out." All eyes were on me. I said, "Well, you'll have to burn me out then." He mumbled something and staggered off. The men assured me that I'd said the right thing, but I'm not so sure.

Fortunately for our peace of mind, his family left Holylands about a month later.

Camp life soon fell into a comfortable and productive routine, which began most mornings chatting with our immediate neighbors, the Donoghues, whose campfire we usually sat at while getting breakfast. Many days ended up back at the same campfire, enjoying further conversation with the Donoghues and passersby. In a letter, George described our routine as winter set in:

> *Dec 5, 1971: The wagon is cold in the morning. I usually stoke up the small wood-burning stove and get back into my sleeping bag until the wagon heats up which considering the small space doesn't take long. The small bunk across the rear of the wagon is just six feet across so my head and toes touch, but I've gotten used to it. The wagon has great atmosphere. It creaks in the wind and you can hear the pitter patter of rain on the canvas roof. Unless the weather is bad, we eat on the wagon steps or at the campfire next door. At first the kids eyeballed my Cheerios as they had never seen boxed cereal before, nor have they eaten grapefruit. We wash up in a plastic dish pan and use the surrounding fields like everyone else for a toilet. There is no rule about which direction men and women go, so you try not to surprise anyone.*
>
> *By late afternoon the men and women return from their rounds and there is usually good conversation around the fires. After dinner, we sit around the campfire again or else go to the pub or sometimes to a movie with Travellers. The pubs are noisy and smoke filled but the atmosphere and conversation are good. I am often able to get people to talk at length about the topics I'm working on. The pubs close at 11, and we're back in camp and in bed by midnight.*

Wanting to know how representative what we were observing at Holylands was of other Travellers in Dublin, we periodically visited other camps in the city. We also frequently attended the weekly meetings in nearby Milltown of Dublin social workers working with Travellers, which enabled us to check our observations against theirs and learn about what was happening in other parts of the city. Late in our fieldwork I was invited to fill in for six weeks for a social worker on leave, which gave me the opportunity to directly experience some of the issues that arise between Travellers and settled Irish in the welfare sphere.

Big John Maughan (left), his cousin Pa, mother, Nan, and brother at their Holylands campfire, 1971.

Katie and Red Mick Connors with their youngest child, Paddy, outside a Dublin church, 1971.

George and I also made short trips to other parts of Ireland to learn about Travellers' situations outside Dublin, and we spent two weeks in England and Scotland visiting local officials dealing with Travellers there as well as visiting some relatives of Holylands' families living in Birmingham.

During the year, we got to know many settled people who were active in the Itinerant Settlement Movement, including its leadership, which was valuable to our research.[6] The friendships we developed with several middle-class Dublin families were especially rewarding. The occasional social evening spent in their homes was not only a pleasant change of scene from camp life but almost always yielded new insights and questions to pursue. They also directed me to teachers, government officials, clerics, physicians, and even scrap metal dealers working with Travellers whom I would later interview.

We also spent many hours in the National Library searching for early historical references to Travellers and in the library of the *Irish Times* going through bulky file folders of newspaper clippings, which often documented clashes over trespassing and efforts to settle Travellers. In the archives of the folklore department at University College Dublin we found a trove of questionnaires about Travellers that had been completed by schoolteachers across Ireland in the early 1950s. These painted a picture of Travellers' work, nomadism, and relationship with the settled community before their urban migration and revealed many of the superstitions and folk beliefs settled people held about them. When either of us felt depressed, anxious, or at loose ends, we could go to one of these places and escape into solitary and productive work. When a complete break from fieldwork was needed, Dublin provided cinemas, theater, museums, art galleries, plays, shops, restaurants, and the zoo—a range of diversions unavailable to anthropologists working in rural villages.

On August 15, 1972, thirteen months after our first conversation with the taxi driver on the way into Dublin from the airport, we left Holylands and Ireland. We had become very close to some families, making our departure emotional on both sides. We promised to return, which we did several times through the mid-1980s. Now, looking back forty years later, we sometimes wonder why they willingly took us into their lives. How many middle-class Irish or American families would put up with two foreigners moving into their neighborhood, watching how they behave, and asking endless questions about their lives? On the other hand, Travellers didn't lose anything by accepting us, and most Holylanders seemed to enjoy—or at least not mind—the novelty of our presence and, I think, appreciated our friendship and the genuine interest and respect we had for their lives.

3

RETURN TO A CHANGING IRELAND

WE RETURNED TO IRELAND IN 2011, EAGER TO RECONNECT WITH THE families we knew and to begin learning how Travellers' lives have changed, but first we had to make it out of the airport. Jet-lagged after a fourteen-hour flight and disoriented by Dublin's new, futuristic terminal, we found our way to the car rental desks only to discover we didn't remember which company we'd booked with. Rebooking at a higher rate, we walked off in the wrong direction and got lost before finally making it to the car pickup area. Obtaining our car, we asked directions to Templeogue, where we'd booked a bed and breakfast, but none of the agency's East European employees knew it. Finally on our way, we merged onto the motorway, heading south through a once-familiar landscape now utterly transformed by a new motorway and commercial development.

At breakfast the next morning, we described our airport debacle to our hostess, who then regaled us with her own story about recent guests who had gotten lost after leaving the airport and driven—to their horror—into a "tinker camp." "Tinkers, knackers," she explained, "that's what we call them." We sat poker-faced as she proceeded to tell us about the Travellers who came to her door asking for water or to use her phone or toilet or who offered to help her "get rid of that old bike" or "tidy up" her back garden—all ruses for robbery, in her opinion. She had grown up on a farm in county Clare and had never trusted Travellers. Now in the city, she never let them past her door. Once some Travellers "just off the boat" from England on their way to a funeral in the countryside had asked to stay, but she had told them she was booked, convinced they would have been too loud for other guests and might steal. "Has anyone ever told them the reasons people are against them is their behavior?" she asked rhetorically. "They're their own worst enemies. Or is everyone just too politically correct to say anything?"

That evening while walking on the footpath along the Dodder River, George fell into conversation with two middle-aged men—one very tall and the other quite short—who picked up on her theme. The tall man's van had been broken into and his carpentry tools stolen. "I live on a cul-de-sac, and they managed to do it in the middle of the day without being seen," he claimed, indicating Travellers' cunning. The short man then recounted the story of an elderly farmer in county Mayo who not long before had shot and killed a trespassing Traveller he suspected of burglary. He was convicted of manslaughter and sentenced to jail, to the outrage of many, but acquitted the following year after an appeal and retrial. When we had left Ireland at the end of our fieldwork in 1972, public sentiment toward Travellers had been softening with growing awareness of the disadvantages and discrimination they faced. Now it seemed that attitudes had hardened again.

The next morning, after buying a cell phone and getting cash from an ATM, we set off for Holylands, our old field site. Nutgrove Avenue, the dirt lane that had cut through an open field leading into the site, is today a paved street that skirts a large shopping mall of the same name. Eight substantial stucco-clad bungalows—a group housing scheme for Travellers— now stand where Holylands' twenty families had once camped in an assortment of caravans, wagons, and shacks. Gone are their horses and carts, scrap metal piles, and campfires as well as the empty field at the top of the site with its scenic view of the Dublin Mountains. A private sports complex now occupies it with new residential neighborhoods stretching beyond. Nutgrove Crescent, as the Travellers' new bungalows have been christened, could easily be mistaken for any residential development if not for the yellow metal barrier straddling the entrance to prevent caravans and large trucks from pulling in.

Driving beneath it, we parked and got out, watchful for aggressive dogs. The houses were well maintained with curtains in the windows and small landscaped front yards, one embellished with trolls, another containing a small shrine to the Virgin Mary, and only two messy with scrap metal. While I walked to the top of the site to see if Dickio and Bridget Connors were home, George struck up a conversation with a woman standing outside. He learned that our good friend Katie Connors had died and that Dickio and Bridget had moved away following the deaths of two children.[1] Two of the other houses were occupied by widows we knew, Nan Connors and Lance Connors, but neither was home.

One of the eight new houses at Nutgrove Crescent, which replaced the old Holylands site, 2011.

Distressed at the bad news and disappointed that no one we knew was around, we decided to move up our visit to the Donoghues, who now lived on the north side of the city. At Holylands we had camped next to Mick and Nan Donoghue and had interacted with members of the family every day. Mick and Nan had died years before, but their daughter Sally lived in local authority housing in Ballymun, an area that in the 1970s had been infamous for crime, much of it occurring in the "Ballymun flats," Ireland's first and only experiment with high-rise public housing. Now, we were to discover, just one tower block remained, and the entire area had undergone a multibillion-euro renewal. Confused by new streets and Ballymun's radically altered appearance, we pulled off the road to phone Sally again for directions. She dispatched her partner, Pat, and son Mush to find us.

Sally had let the family know we were coming, and everyone living nearby, including her brother Kevin and his wife, Trish, were there to greet us. The living room was small but cozy, its walls covered with photographs, including a collage created from George's images from our time at Holylands. It felt good to be surrounded by old friends and our shared memories of the past. When we had known Sally in the 1970s, she had just given birth to Nanzer, her first child. Since then she'd given birth fourteen more times (including a son she'd named

Sally Donoghue and her mother, Nan, look after Sally's new daughter, Nanzer, 1972.

A Travelling family on the road in county Dublin, 1972.

after George) and now had thirty-four grandchildren. They were surprised to learn we had only one son, Morgan, and that he was not yet married.

We were very interested in learning what impact settlement was having on Travellers and how they viewed themselves. Sally was an interesting, and somewhat atypical, case since she'd actually spent her formative years—two to sixteen—living under "settled" circumstances in a convent orphanage. An unknown number of children were taken from Travelling parents and placed in care over the years, including Sally and four of her siblings. Rejoining Nan and Mick after her release, she had moved with them to England and lived in a flat for a few years before returning to Ireland and a life on the road. Back in Dublin, Sally had met and married Billy Flanaghan, a working-class Dubliner who was alienated from his family. Despite these strong connections to settled life, Sally identifies as a Traveller and idealizes a nomadic life she barely experienced. "Even if I'd known what hardship was [in store]," she told me, sounding remarkably like her mother, Nan, "if there was a big field

there and I had a blanket . . . I'd still want to come back as a Traveller . . . to have freedom and a whole load of Travelling children."

Her brother Kevin, who had been raised as a Traveller and never separated from his parents, had also married a non-Traveller and had brought up his six children as settled people, although they are fully aware of his background. He enjoys the comforts of his house and garden but also views traveling with nostalgia. "My heart goes out when I see this," he said, holding a photograph of his brother Michael and Anthony Maughan lying in the grass on the roadside in county Wicklow.

> *I love that life—living free. Living in this house, I'm trapped. On the road you wake up in the morning and you lift the front of the tent. The breeze blows in and you see your mother out there putting clothes on the line or over the hedges. You don't have to get up to go anywhere. You can do what you want. That's freedom. I'd love to go back to the road, but it's not the same. We didn't appreciate it then. We didn't know what we had.*

That night at dinner with Mervyn Ennis, a social worker who had begun working with Travellers in the mid-1970s, we talked about the emergence of Traveller activism—one of the most significant developments since our departure. During our fieldwork, few Travellers had any formal education. Preoccupied with making ends meet, they also lacked the time or perspective to think about the bigger picture, about Travellers as an "ethnic minority" or about discrimination and civil rights. Now virtually all Travelling children are in school, although most leave early. Some 69 percent of the Traveller population today has been educated through primary level, and a small number of Travellers are going on to higher education. Accompanying this educational change has been the growing ability of Travellers to speak for themselves. Today, several national Traveller-run organizations as well as dozens of local groups work to better their lives through literacy classes and health initiatives, youth and cultural awareness projects, political action and media campaigns. Individual Travellers are also far more aware of their legal rights and of their shared identity as Travellers.

As we got up to leave, Mervyn handed us a printed wedding invitation he'd just received from a Traveller. We'd never met the future bride, Martina Connors, but we had known her mother, Maggie, and her late father, Bun Connors. The first Traveller wedding we attended, the day after our arrival in 1971, had been that of Bun's son Jim—Martina's much older half-brother. At the time, news of a Traveller wedding spread by word of mouth and nearly all relatives were invited, although not all would be close enough to attend. The printed invitation Mervyn held, with the wedding and reception for invited guests only, was a real departure. It signaled both the bride's sophistication and perhaps her desire, the three of us concluded, to avoid conflict by controlling who attended the event. Mervyn knew that she was marrying outside the group, far outside—to a young man from Bangladesh—and that not all Travellers approved. We later received our own invitation. It seemed incredible that our first Traveller wedding and probably our last would be those of two siblings forty years apart.

Before leaving Dublin the next morning to begin our journey around Ireland, we picked up Carolyn Hou, one of two anthropology students who would be assisting us during the summer. She had just arrived from London, where she'd spent the past year as an exchange student, and was staying at a B&B downtown. Then we dropped by Scratch Films to say hello to filmmaker Liam McGrath, who had used some of George's photographs in two documentaries he had made about Travellers: *Southpaw,* about Francis Barrett, the first Traveller to box in the Olympics, and *Blood of the Travellers,* which explored what recent DNA research revealed about their origins. Serendipity places a huge role in research, as it does in life. It had been George's loan of photographs to Mervyn for possible use as illustrations in a book he was writing that had resulted in the library exhibit that had drawn such an enthusiastic response from Travellers a few months earlier. Now, unbeknownst to us, George's loan of photographs to Liam would lead to a development that would dramatically alter the shape of our summer research.

After a quick tour of his studio and offices, we sat down with Liam to chat while his assistant Orla Malone made copies of his documentaries and some other footage for us. We described our summer plans and were soon back in the car heading south to county Carlow, where we planned to see Josey Connors and Francie O'Leary. Josey had been a pretty and outgoing twelve-year-old when we lived at Holylands, her cousin Francie an adventurous eighteen-year-old. Now married for thirty-five years, they were the parents of twelve grown children. And although we hadn't seen them since leaving Holylands, we remembered them well and had been in touch indirectly through e-mail with their daughter Selina, a successful singer and university student.

TULLOW, COUNTY CARLOW

Following disconcertingly vague directions, we pulled up in front of a yellow bungalow on the outskirts of Tullow, a prosperous market town. A small shrine to the Virgin Mary in the front garden and a trailer barely visible at the end of a long driveway suggested we were

The O'Learys examine photographs from the 1970s in their comfortable living room, 2011.

at the right place. But no one seemed to be home or answered the only cell phone number we had. As we sat in the car wondering what to do, a man walked up. Balding with a bit of a belly, we assumed he was a neighbor, but as soon as we lowered the window he shouted, "Welcome, George and Sharon." Now fifty-eight, Francie as might be expected looked entirely different. We got out, shook hands warmly, and followed him down the driveway and into the house. Josey arrived soon after, and for the next several hours we sat at their large kitchen table looking through photographs, joined by daughters, sons, grandchildren, and Josey's mother, Lance, who was visiting. Carolyn dutifully described the encounter in her first field note:

> There was an instant connection between them—the anthropologists and the Travellers. I noticed that S and J often touched one another on the shoulder. Talking was easy and comfortable, like dear old friends getting together after a long absence. There was talk of S and G's wagon and horse, the soccer team G started, the book Sharon wrote about Nan.[2] Josey commented with some seriousness that G and S had changed her life—for example, she bought a toothbrush after she saw them use it. S had told her to brush her teeth twice a day. Josey showed her teeth, still pearly white. She also mentioned that S and G had introduced all the families at Holylands to grapefruit, popcorn, and boxed cereal, which J said she found hilarious because she thought the cereal was food for chickens. Josey's daughters had no idea what anthropologists did, so I wondered what they were thinking Sharon and George were doing living in the camp all those years ago.

The O'Learys' large home was well maintained, as were most of the Traveller homes we would visit. It was also well appointed. The kitchen has granite countertops and high-end appliances. The living room has matching plush sofas, a display of Royal Crown Derby china, crystal chandeliers, and a fifty-two-inch Samsung flat-screen TV. The family's living situation is emblematic of two of the most visible and dramatic changes in Traveller life since the early 1970s, namely their settlement and comparative affluence. Most of the Travellers we would visit are much better off today than they had been and now live much more comfortable lives. Several told us with only slight overstatement, "There are no more poor Travellers today." Certainly the poverty and material deprivation—lack of running water, electricity, and toilets—that families endured in the 1970s are no longer issues for the great majority who are now housed, although some families struggle to pay all their bills and many of those in caravans still live in overcrowded conditions.

Ireland's final push toward settling Travellers came with the Housing Act of 1998, which required local governments to accommodate all the Travelling families in their area by 2005. Today, 86 percent of Traveller families live in permanent structures: in a local authority housing estate like Sally Donoghue Flanaghan does; in a group housing scheme for Travellers like Nutgrove Crescent, which replaced the old Holylands site; in a privately owned home like that purchased by the O'Learys; or in rented houses and flats. The minority still living in caravans do so mostly on local authority–built "halting sites"—serviced trailer parks for Travellers. Legislation passed in 2002 now makes it a criminal offense to camp on public or private land, punishable by a month in jail, a three-thousand-euro fine, and the confiscation of property. As a result of all this, it is no longer possible for Travelling People living in Ireland to pursue a life "on the road."

We sat at the O'Learys' table into the early evening, fortified by refills of coffee and tea and later by wine. The photographs sparked intense interest. A priority with all the Travellers we met, regardless of their age or gender, was to correctly identify every adult and child visible in an image. At times this resulted in heated arguments and once, weeks later in Finglas, a wager among a group of men when the identity of one young woman was unclear. When a positive identification wasn't possible, Travellers usually narrowed it down with a comment like, "It's a McDonagh; you can tell by the eyes."

Boys at Holylands play with a pet cockerel, 1972.

Margaret Connors gets water from Holylands' only tap, 1972.

Josey and Francie laughed at early images of themselves. Looking at a photograph of children clowning around at Holylands, Josey recalled her own childhood:

> The children then had more freedom. They were always outside until they were called for supper or bedtime. There were always games. I remember playing cowboys and Indians, skip, and house. We didn't have much like television, computers, and laptops. I had a very happy childhood growing up. I don't remember being deprived of very much. You didn't expect a lot, so you didn't miss it. We always had food and there was always music, and that was enough.

We also remembered Josey's hard work. As the family's eldest daughter, she had helped look after her many younger brothers and sisters, prepare meals, fetch water, get "messages" (run errands), and clean. Boys like Francie, although responsible for the horses and helping collect scrap metal, had a much easier life. After looking at more photographs revealing camp conditions—including many dirty faces and crowded muddy places—Josey concluded, "It *was* a rough life."

Meanwhile her mother, Lance, now in her mid-seventies and hampered by diabetes and failing eyesight, had trouble making out many people in the images and identifying the various children. She had been one of Holylands' younger married women during our fieldwork—a highly visible yet distant figure living at the top of the site, totally occupied with the tasks of caring for her large family. "Me mother used to wash clothes for thirteen children from one tap stuck to a tree," Josey said pointing to an image of Holylands in 1972.

> You can imagine all the work she did all day, and in the evening she would have to wash our vessels and our clothes. We didn't take much notice of what she was doing. I wouldn't be able to do it. There's no way I could do all that now—I'd be half dead. If my mother had a washing machine years ago, it would have made life easy. If she had even basic things like hot water, imagine the comfort she would have had. What I remember of my mother then is loads of children around and all these big pots—we were always being fed.

"Lance has over one hundred grandchildren and great grandchildren," Carolyn wrote that evening in her field notes. "When G and S asked her to reckon them, she could only remember 13 of her 16 kids. Can you have so many kids that it's hard to keep track of them?" With Josey's help, Lance had tried to tally up her grandchildren but could account for only eighty-four. Together they puzzled over who was missing. Carolyn was stunned when we told her later that Lance had actually given birth twenty-nine times. When we lived at Holylands, Lance already had thirteen children, but her reproductive career was not over.

Demographic research in the 1970s found that Travellers were the second most fertile population then studied, after Hutterites, with an average of ten pregnancies per woman. At the time, Travellers did not know about birth control; the church had deemed it immoral, and the state had made its importation and sale illegal. Consequently, social workers never mentioned it to Travellers, and even settled Irish who wanted to use birth control had to obtain it surreptitiously or leave the country to purchase a supply. Large families were also valued within Traveller culture, in part for the enhanced reputation and status they gave men. Once Travellers began collecting social assistance benefits, each dependent child under sixteen increased a family's income with weekly "Unemployment Assistance" and monthly "Children's Allowance" payments.[3]

Attitudes toward birth control and family size have since changed. As our journey progressed, I found that many Traveller women's groups now help women obtain birth control and that families are smaller, although still larger than those of non-Travellers. While Lance had twenty-nine pregnancies and sixteen surviving children and Josey had given birth fourteen times and has twelve surviving children, Josey's daughters said they wanted no more than five children. Yet some resistance to birth control remains. After another Travelling woman described her birth control use to me later in our journey, she whispered, "If my husband knew, it'd be *thwack* [punching her fist into the palm of her hand]."

Sadly, life expectancy is one demographic that has not changed much in the last forty years, despite the significant material improvement in Travellers' lives. All of the adult men we had known at Holylands in the early 1970s are now dead. Josey's father, Big Jim, was among them, dying at fifty. When Josey found his face in the background of a wedding photograph, she reflected on the loss: "I miss my father. I miss his advice. If there was a problem you would go and ask him. He was a great storyteller and a real gentle man with the children. But he was very shy. I wouldn't think you'll have many other photos of my father." She was right; we didn't.

As we looked through more photographs, Carolyn noticed "how much time was spent talking about death. Almost every photo Josey looked at, she'd mention if that person had passed away or was ill. She said it bluntly—'He's dead.' 'He's dead many years.' 'She's gone.' 'He's dead too.' 'She died last year.' 'He's in a bad way.' It was all matter of fact." Unfortunately, it *is* a matter of fact. A study of Traveller health conducted in 2010 found that the average life expectancy for Traveller men is sixty-one, or fifteen fewer years than for other Irish men. The life expectancy for Traveller women today is seventy, or eleven fewer years than that of other Irish women.[4] One-third of Travelling men die of "external causes," notably alcohol and suicide. We would hear much about both topics in coming days.

Men from Holylands gather in front of the Church of the Good Shepherd
in Churchtown, Dublin, for a wedding, 1971. Josey's father, "Big Jim Connors", is in the center;
Francie O'Leary leans against the wall on the right.

While at the O'Learys', we were struck by the strong interest their children showed in the photographs and in learning more about their family. Josey's daughters wanted copies and two of them gave us their addresses, in stage whispers making us promise to send the prints directly to them so they could not be claimed by other family members. We thought of our own son, who was their age but who had little of their curiosity about past generations. This interest in old photographs and family history was repeated over and over with the other Travellers we would meet, and not just among those to whom we had a prior connection and who might, therefore, be expected to show interest.

Anthony Maughan riding in traffic, 1972. In the 1970s, Traveller horses sometimes wandered into traffic, causing accidents. Anthony may have caused this one.

Travellers often noticed small details in the images that had escaped us. Francie, for example, while looking at a photograph of Anthony Maughan riding a horse through traffic, pointed out the automobile accident in the background—a car had stopped and there was broken glass on the pavement. We both liked this image but had never paid close attention to the background before. Other Travellers commented on details of material culture, such as the quality of the tack sported by our mare, Franny, or the craftsmanship evident in a barrel-top wagon. This attention to detail reveals something about Traveller culture, especially true when they lived on the road and supported large families by their skills and wits. People had to pay careful attention and remember details of their surroundings, both to take advantage of opportunities and to avoid pitfalls. Being illiterate also places a premium on observation and memory. This may explain behavior that some non-Travellers find disconcerting, namely the overtly investigatory manner in which Travellers survey new surroundings, even a job site where they are seeking work. It creates suspicion.

The next morning while checking our e-mail at Tullow's library before leaving town, we received a phone call from Liam McGrath. He had been thinking about our conversation and research and wanted to know if we would consider letting him make a documentary about our journey. He thought using our early fieldwork photographs to prompt Travellers to talk about change could make an interesting film, one that would raise important issues that had been outside the scope of his previous films. Almost without hesitation George said, "Why not?" Liam said he'd drive down the next day to Kilkenny, where we were headed, so that we could talk about the idea.

KILKENNY, COUNTY KILKENNY

Kilkenny is a vibrant town on the River Nore with a prominent and picturesque thirteenth-century castle, a lively pub scene, and music and arts festivals that make it a popular tourist and Irish holiday destination. One of the first things we noticed upon arrival, however, was the Roma (Gypsy) woman sitting on the sidewalk in front of a bookshop on High Street. In the 1970s, she would have been a Travelling woman, although only some families had begged on the streets. It had been considered disreputable behavior by families who classified themselves as "respectables"—something that only "roughs" did. But even self-defined respectables had not hesitated to go door to door in suburban neighborhoods seeking "a little bit of help." Today some Travelling women continue to visit their "ladies" or regular "call backs" in the suburbs. We had been reminded of Travellers' sensitivity to status distinctions and their concern with reputation the previous day when George, while talking to Francie about social change, had asked him if any Travellers still begged on the street. Francie had been quick to remind him that the O'Learys and Connorses had *never* done so.

Seeing a Roma in Kilkenny was yet another sign of Ireland's new population diversity, much of it taking place during the country's economic boom or "Celtic Tiger" years (mid-1990s–2007). Today there are an estimated five thousand Roma in Ireland, most from Romania but also from the Czech Republic, Slovakia, Hungary, Poland, and Bulgaria. The same period also saw the arrival of refugees and asylum seekers from Africa, Eastern Europe, and other countries. Today, 17 percent of Ireland's population is foreign-born. In the 1970s, the Travelling People were Ireland's only noticeable minority.

While waiting for Liam, we split up to poke around town. In Kilkenny's library I pulled Mícheál MacGréil's *Prejudice in Ireland Revisited* from the shelf to peruse it once again. It compared the results of two national surveys—conducted in 1972 and 1988—of Irish attitudes toward different social groups and categories.[5] Between the two surveys the "social distance" between Travellers and the general Irish population had grown. More recent research shows even less acceptance of Travellers. In a large-scale study conducted in 2007 by Roland Tormey and Jim Gleeson, large majorities of the post-primary students they surveyed reported feeling no social distance from black African immigrants (74 percent) or from Eastern Europeans or Muslims (64 percent in both cases), but only 27 percent felt this way about Travellers.[6] Moreover, 42 percent of the students reported feeling "high" or "very high" levels of social distance from Travellers. That Irish Travellers are now more alien to settled Irish than are Africans and other recent immigrants is hard to imagine.

Meanwhile, George visited the Book Centre, where we'd seen the Roma woman begging. Despite being a large bookshop specializing in Irish-interest titles, it did not have a single book on Travellers. "There really isn't any interest in them," the clerk maintained; "they're kind of settled and invisible now, except when there's a big row." Discussing this later among ourselves, we were not sure his assertion was altogether true. There was evidence, including the popularity of Liam's two films about Travellers, to suggest that interest remained. But clearly, the relationship between Travellers and large segments of the general population was a troubled one.

That evening we met Liam in the hotel coffee shop to talk about his ideas for a documentary and what the logistics might entail. The next morning he filmed short interviews with each of us, including Carolyn. We then parted, with Liam returning to Dublin to find out about funding and our continuing on to Cork where we had made plans to show our photographs to several Traveller groups and to connect with Aisling Kearns, our second student research assistant. An Irish American, Aisling would be staying with relatives in Cork while interning—we hoped—with a Traveller organization.

4

CORK

LIKE THE REST OF IRELAND, CORK'S HISTORY RUNS DEEP. THE CITY BEGAN as a monastic settlement in the sixth century, became a Norse trading port in the tenth, was invaded by the Normans in the twelfth, and was colonized by the English in the sixteenth before achieving political independence—along with the rest of Ireland—in the twentieth. Today it is Ireland's second largest urban area and a global pharmaceutical and IT center as well as a popular tourist destination. Cork is an attractive city originally built on islands in an estuary, with more than twenty bridges crossing the River Lee's two channels. Since we planned to stay a week, we moved into an efficiency apartment located across the street from University College Cork. After settling in, we walked around the campus. It was sunny, and the university's lawns shimmered with the same intense green as the Irish countryside we'd just driven through, making it hard to believe that not that long before, they'd been under three feet of water after severe winter storms.

The next morning, after Carolyn and Aisling arrived to begin transcribing our interview tapes, George and I set off for Fitzgerald Park to see the Cork Public Museum's new exhibit on Traveller culture, the only permanent exhibit of its kind in Ireland.[1] The exhibit represents Travellers through historical photographs and material culture from life on the road—a barrel-top wagon, a bender tent and flat cart, and tools of the trade for which Travellers are best known, tinsmithing. Developed by the Cork Travelling Women's Network, it turned out to be one of many examples of Travelling women taking the lead in cultural heritage projects and outreach to the settled community.

A Holylands mother washes her children. The trailer's broken window suggests a domestic dispute, 1972.

In the 1970s few women had the opportunity to be involved in anything other than caring for their large families. In most households men were the dominant force, although change was stirring for Travelling women, in Dublin at least. They had begun collecting the Children's Allowance, which, unlike the "dole" or Unemployment Assistance that men received, was kept and spent by women. This income, added to what they earned going door to door in the suburbs soliciting food, clothing, and small amounts of cash, not only contributed to the maintenance of the household but also enhanced their authority within it.

In the city, women also acted as cultural brokers or "gatekeepers" when Travellers dealt with outsiders. Whenever a social worker, Itinerant Settlement Committee volunteer, or nun or lay religious person arrived in camp, it was a woman who stepped forward to negotiate the interaction. Since these visits often concerned children's education, health, or spiritual welfare,

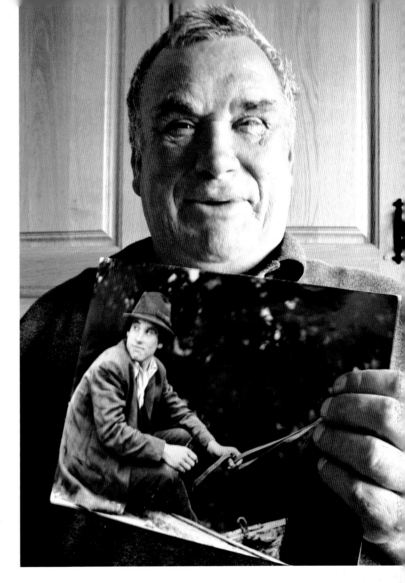

Pa Maughan holds a photograph of himself as a fifteen-year-old, 2011.

both sides saw this as appropriate. But women also blocked interaction between Travelling men and unwelcome outsiders like the police. Ironically, it was women's lower status at the time and relative powerlessness vis-à-vis men that helped them keep inquisitive outsiders at bay, since they could feign ignorance of their husbands' affairs or legitimately claim that they lacked the ability to make the decisions or provide the information being asked of them.

Anne Connors examines photographs from the early 1970s with other members of her family in 2011. An enlargement she had made of George's photograph of her parents hangs on the wall.

By the 1980s a few Travelling women had gained national attention as early activists. Rosella McDonald—with legal representation by Mary Robinson, who later became president of Ireland, and help from Traveller supporters like Mervyn Ennis—challenged the legality of the Dublin county council's eviction practices. The Supreme Court's landmark ruling in her favor required local authorities from then on to provide Travelling families with alternative accommodations or camping sites before the authorities could evict them. In 1982 Nan Joyce, a poised and articulate woman who had lived at Holylands for several months during our fieldwork, ran for a seat in Dáil Éireann, the lower house of parliament, and, although losing, received more votes than her main opponent, who had run on a racist anti-Traveller ticket. Today Travelling women have a much greater voice and independence, both within their families and outside. Paddy "Pa" Maughan, whom we knew as a teenager and who is now the father of seven, was just one of many men to tell us, "Women are the bosses of everything today."

The next day Liam and a three-person crew (sound, camera, and logistics coordinator) arrived in Cork and that evening shot some footage of typical research activities: George and me dictating field notes and Carolyn and Aisling transcribing interviews. Nothing was scripted. Liam favors an observational approach to filmmaking. There was no time for a script anyway; it had been less than a week since he hit upon the idea of making a documentary. Our own research plan was open-ended as well. We simply wanted to meet as many Travellers as we could—both those we knew and new people—show them our photographs from the 1970s, and prompt them to talk. The crew would follow us around as we did this, but Liam also knew some Travellers from his earlier films whom he wanted us to meet. As filmmakers, both he and co-director Kim Bartley had to think visually in order to get the range of images they would need to tell the story. From this point on, our time and many activities were worked out in collaboration with the film crew.

The next morning we drove to a small community center and group housing scheme for Travellers in Mahon on the south side of the city. It was actually a joint group housing scheme that had been built for two extended family groupings—the Keenans and the O'Reillys. For years they had camped nearby in a large field before being displaced when the land was developed into the Mahon Point Shopping Center, Cork's largest. This visit was our first attempt to coordinate the activities of the crew, ourselves, and our two student research assistants. Despite having GPS, our three-car caravan got terribly lost, and we arrived nearly an hour late. We were warmly greeted, nevertheless, by the Travelling women and social workers who had been waiting for us and were shown around the community center before sitting down to discuss our twin projects—our photo elicitation research and the crew's filming of it.

In conversation later, George asked Bridget Carmody, the center's impressive Traveller director, how leaving the road and settling in houses was affecting Traveller identity. "While I'm a Traveller," she replied,

> I have one sister who no longer sees herself as a Traveller. She's happy to deny who she is, and she can't understand why I'm pushing it—why no matter where I go, I say, "I'm a Traveller." I don't know how this happened because we both come from the same family. We were both reared the same way, both raised in a house, but we are completely different on this matter. Maybe I just had more of an interest in our culture.

I think it is also discrimination. Some people like my sister just don't want to deal with it. My sister will say, "I'm not putting my children through that." Whereas I'll fight it. She married a Traveller who didn't identify himself as a Traveller either, whereas my husband does. I live in a group housing scheme where everyone is a Traveller, and my children don't have to hide who they are when they're at home. My sister lives in a normal housing estate where she is the only Traveller there.

My children have always been taught to be proud of who they are, even though they don't know what it's like to travel. They are very proud of the museum [in Cork], of the room, and of the wagon [which her husband built]. My son went on a school tour to the museum, and Stella, the museum curator, recognized him and talked to him. He brought the class up and said, "My daddy built this," and, "My mommy was one of the coordinators of this." My kids can say, "That's my picture on the wall. That's my daddy's picture on the wall." My sister's children haven't got that, and when they go to the museum they walk around the room like a settled child. But I wouldn't ram it back my sister's throat and say, "You are a Traveller. Don't deny who you are." That's people's choice. It's my choice to tell people that I am a Traveller and proud to be one—to be part of Ireland but different at the same time.

Discrimination clearly plays an important role in individual Travellers' calculations of the cost and benefits of openly identifying as a Traveller. Back in Dublin at the end of our trip, two former Holylanders who had both become successful businessmen declined to appear in Liam's film for fear of losing their non-Traveller clients.

"There was more of a community before," one of the women said as she shuffled through our photographs. "Everybody knew everyone, and there was less feuding." We told them that some of the housed Travellers we'd talked to in Dublin claimed that they'd love to go back on the road. "Do you think they really would?" George asked. "Most definitely," Bridget responded as others nodded. "But I personally wouldn't," she continued.

It's not something that I ever experienced or would take to, but the majority of Travellers would say yes. They'd love to be able—even if only in the summer—to get into a trailer and go. Leave their worries behind.

Today, Travellers are in such enclosed space. That's why there are a lot of the feuds. If you have an argument with someone, you can't pack up your trailer and leave. You're stuck there. And then it just escalates and escalates into a full-blown feud. Travellers can't move away and don't know what to do in the situation. Then the stress builds up, and everyone begins picking at each other. It could be anything—his great-grandfather was fighting with the other fella's great-grandfather. The younger generation is holding grudges, and they don't even know what they're really about—how they started. It just traveled down through the family.

There was a time when they would have a fair fight and the best man would win. They'd shake hands, and that would be the end of it. But that's not happening anymore. Travellers can't handle losing. It's all-out war, with the whole family and their friends out fighting. And there's more weapons now than the older generation had. Now they're using knives, and in some places people are getting shot.

A portion of the Spring Lane site, county Cork, seen from above in 2011.

"Can a group like yours do anything to defuse the situation?" we asked. "Very little," replied Bridget:

> As an organization we can't get involved. We're stuck between a rock and a hard place. Whose side would you take? Who do you say is right and who is wrong? Personally, as a Traveller, I wouldn't dream of getting involved in another family's feud. It's nothing to do with you. You stare a bit, and then you mind your own business. If the women were dealing with it, it would never happen. But they haven't got a lot of choice; they just have to live with the men's feuds and carry on.

The Mahon Travellers' and social workers' support for our research and the filming was due, in part, to their already having some of George's photographs displayed on the walls of their community center. Their respect for Liam's recently broadcast *Blood of the Travellers* documentary—so unlike the then popular "reality" television series *My Big Fat Gypsy Wedding*, which they despised—also helped enormously. When we returned the next day to film

Sharon and Kieran McCarthy examine photographs at Spring Lane, 2011.

and talk some more, one woman struck me as particularly thoughtful, and before leaving Cork I returned to interview her privately. Kathleen Keenan's narrative makes up chapter 5.

After finishing at Mahon, we next went to Spring Lane, an official site located in an abandoned quarry in Ballyvolane, on the northern edge of Cork. It was a pleasant setting—at least in good weather—with open space next to a soccer pitch where families grazed their horses, but it was also very crowded. Built in 1988 as a temporary site for ten families, it now held thirty and looked it, with trailers, washrooms, sheds, and stables jigsawed together. Virtually everyone was a McCarthy. We had never met them before, and at first they found it difficult to believe that we had once owned a horse and barrel-top wagon and lived with Travellers. As we tried explaining what anthropologists do, one man spied a photograph of me making dinner over a campfire with our barrel-top wagon in the background. "Is that you?" he exclaimed incredulously, calling others over to have a look. When they learned that we were also interested in taking new photographs to illustrate how Travelling life had changed, most became eager subjects.

As we talked with people, Aisling and Carolyn explored the site. Watching them reminded me of my earliest experiences with Travellers when I was not much older—the eagerness yet awkwardness of engaging strangers in conversation, the emotional challenge of coping with evasiveness or outright dismissal, the sensation of being overwhelmed when surrounded by clamoring children.

Late in the afternoon as we prepared to leave, Kieran McCarthy took Liam aside to ask if he'd bring the film crew back after dinner to photograph his collection of old kettles, cooking pots, and griddles. Kieran had shown them to me earlier, and I'd been surprised and pleased to find a Travelling man so proud of these pieces of his heritage. Liam agreed, mostly out of courtesy. But when he returned, he was met by a group of men with their horses hitched to sulkies, waiting to race for the camera. The crew obliged and filmed them on the surrounding streets, their fast-trotting horses passing surprised motor-

A McCarthy girl practices her footwork while the film crew works in the background, 2011.

ists, hooves clattering sharply on the pavement in the golden light of early evening. Afterward, Kieran told Liam he had a small camping trailer that we could use if we wanted to stay on the site a few nights. From Liam's point of view, it was a good idea. It would evoke our early research and give the crew more opportunity to capture scenes of everyday Traveller life, and it would also give us time when the crew wasn't around to talk to people. When we told Aisling and Carolyn, they were enthusiastic, if a bit intimidated.

Returning from school, Martin McCarthy fends off a mock attack from a cousin, 2011.

Three-year-old Kathleen McCarthy with two of her family's ponies, 2011.

Being on the site around the clock, even for so short a period, did allow us to blend into the background a bit and to experience the ebb and flow of daily life. It brought back vivid memories of waking up at Holylands, listening to the transition from the quiet of early morning, when birdsong and the intermittent cries of children were the only sounds to be heard, to the full chorus of chickens, dogs, horses, people, lorries, and general camp life. We were awoken our first morning by five-year-old Martin McCarthy, eager to show us his pony. Martin visited many times throughout our stay to watch what we were doing but also in his self-appointed role as protector. Whenever other children entered the yard where the

Aisling Kearns and Carolyn Hou
in the camping trailer we shared
at Spring Lane, 2011.

small caravan we were staying in was parked, Martin boldly ordered them out: "When my father's not here, I'm the boss of this yard!" Like the Travelling children we remembered from the 1970s, young Martin was a precocious mix of aggressiveness and innocent charm. Other occurrences also brought back memories of living at Holylands, including a police car silently cruising through the site each day.

On our second evening we crowded into Kieran and Briddie McCarthy's trailer to watch a DVD copy of the previous evening's sulky racing footage. As flames flickered in the trailer's gas fireplace, Briddie stood at the kitchen counter making sandwiches and tea while twelve of us crowded around their television to watch. And watch we did—three times. The intensity with which Kieran and his sons focused on the screen and their obvious pleasure underscored the importance of horses in their lives. To everyone's relief, three-year-old Kathleen, who had been lying on the sofa intermittently kicking the TV, causing the image to break up, finally got up and left the trailer. She returned about a half hour later, towel draped over her head and her pajamas on backwards, asking for a rack (comb). She had just bathed, washed her hair, and dressed herself for bed. I could not imagine any three-year-old American child I knew doing the same.

At Spring Lane, Carolyn and Aisling got a taste of participant observation. While they were upbeat, there were also some uncomfortable moments. Carolyn, a Taiwanese American, wasn't sure how to react to remarks made by some young men and boys who called her "Chinny" or asked, "How can you see out of those slanty eyes?" Were they mocking her? Were they intentionally trying to hurt her feelings? Did their racist comments indicate a naïveté about difference? Or were they just a reflection of Travellers' characteristic bluntness? Both Carolyn and Aisling dealt with suggestive sexual comments they did not always understand and some inappropriate touching. One teenager grabbed Carolyn from behind and tried to lift up her skirt; another pinched her. Neither girl knew how indignant or angry they could be without spoiling the research we were all trying to do. Things became easier after Kieran's young daughters took them under their wing, advising them to avoid all boys and young men and to steer clear of the site's campfire at night, which was a male domain. I learned later from Briddie that Kieran was losing sleep worrying about them and also felt responsible for our welfare and the safety of our possessions.

Most young married women and girls at Spring Lane stayed indoors after dark, attending to domestic chores and watching television. A few unmarried women in their twenties who had their own cars had the freedom to go out, but when on the site none of the women mixed much with the men, even though they were related to most. At Holylands in the 1970s, mixed groups routinely sat around the campfires at night and couples went to the pubs together, although there was gender segregation in other ways. Women carefully avoided being around unrelated men, even if their children were present, and were cautious about whom they talked to for fear of arousing their husbands' jealousy. Parents closely monitored their daughters' activities.

More youths now appear to challenge adult authority openly. At Spring Lane I watched several adolescents kicking a soccer ball alarmingly close to a group of men who were talking nearby. When one of the men—an uncle—finally told them to stop, they got angry and challenged him to make them. "That's something that would never have happened forty years ago," I muttered to Margaret McCarthy, who was standing with me watching. She agreed and to my chagrin instantly yelled out, "Lads, listen. Sharon says that never would have happened years ago. She's right, too." Earlier I'd watched a five-year-old who'd been bullying young Martin refuse to obey his uncle's command to stop and go away. Instead, he yelled back and wouldn't budge. But we also met extremely well behaved and respectful Travelling children in Cork and elsewhere.

Staying on the site created opportunities for lengthy private conversations. As parents, Briddie and Kieran McCarthy's big concern was keeping their children out of trouble. They kept close watch over their fourteen- and eleven-year-old daughters and kept their two teenage sons busy. None of the young men and boys on the site had regular work, so keeping busy usually meant caring for horses and playing sports. Boxing is hugely popular among

Patrick McCarthy, winner of many boxing trophies, practices in his family's makeshift gym at the Spring Lane site, 2011.

Travellers. Several families had created small gyms inside wooden sheds or metal cargo containers. Here men and boys worked out with punching bags, lifted weights, and skipped rope. They were places, like the site's nightly campfire, where males of all ages hung out. The McCarthy boys had already won several All Ireland boxing championships; their trophies, medals, and certificates covered the walls and shelves of the tiny bedroom they shared in their parents' caravan. Younger men and boys on the site also played handball and soccer, swam, and jogged in the early evening—the latter two were unheard-of activities for the Travellers we knew in the 1970s. Several girls on the site also played soccer and ran. Young men talked about the importance of getting a good workout to relieve boredom and reduce the tensions that build up hanging around the camp all day with little to do. We'd never heard Travellers articulate such views before, although sports had always been important to them. It was one of many small signs of how much less isolated and marginalized from mainstream society Travellers are today.

At Spring Lane, horses rivaled, if not eclipsed, sports in their importance to many men. Small stables dotted the site, mixed in with family gyms. An adjacent field provided grazing, which the men supplemented, at some expense, with purchased hay. "Horses are like family," Kieran explained. "We have to have horses. It's in the blood going back generations. We loves horses. Having horses around keeps us happy. Being able to drive a cob, take him out for a spin, is a great relief if you have the depression or the stress. They [local authority] want to house us, but it's no good if we can't keep a pony. You know what I mean? We have to have a horse. They're like family." George asked if boys feel the same way as their fathers and uncles do about horses. "Yes, because they're reared up with horses. That's why we have small miniature ponies for the kids, to keep their interest. My Martin [five-year-old son] loves his pony. He spends many hours every day with him. When his pony was taken to the horse pound [picked up by the police for straying], he wouldn't go to school for three days

Boys at Spring Lane play football on the sports field adjacent to the site, 2011.

Five-year-old Martin McCarthy (right) feeds his pony each morning in his family's stable, 2011.

until it was out of the pound." But Travellers' ability to keep horses is under attack. "If they [settled society] had their way," Paddy McCarthy asserted, "they'd take all the horses away. They'd put us in a way where we wouldn't be able to keep a horse. Just last weekend now, they [police] took four animals. The fine is very steep, €250. We had to put our money together to get out the ponies. They took us off the road, and now they're trying to take our horses away too. They're trying to make it difficult every way they can. They just wants Travellers to wear out and disappear."

Most of the horses Travellers keep are heavy-boned draft animals with piebald or skew-bald coloring, although lighter-boned horses are kept for sulky racing. Throughout our stay we watched boys muck out stalls and water, feed, wash, groom, and lead their animals out

The McCarthy boys at the Spring Lane site, 2011.

to graze in the nearby field or soccer pitch. They also rode their horses up and down the laneways of the site. It was obvious that horses kept boys busy and made them less likely to get in trouble. They also taught responsibility. Men's affection for and pride in their animals was evident in the frequent requests George received to photograph their horses: boys riding bareback, men showing off an animal's feathering or folding back a mare's lips to expose her teeth, or, in one instance, a father placing six young children together on the back of his seventeen-hand mare.

Horses are central to many men's identity as Travellers. "Travelling men are very old-fashioned," explained Bridget Carmody. "They're trying to hold on to their horses when it's just no longer possible with us being in houses. Some say it's in our culture. Some say it's in our blood. They've known nothing else. Without horses, it's just boredom for the men, and that has a lot to do with the physical violence as well." Most Travellers today, outside the small number living on sites like Spring Lane, have no place to keep an animal. Renting a field for grazing is difficult and expensive. Even for those who have space, like the McCarthys, horses are costly: hay and feed alone run thirty euros per horse per week, and any horses caught wandering are impounded, with expensive fines and pound fees.

Some link the dramatic increase in suicide among Traveller men to the boredom and depression they feel because of the breakdown of their former way of life, including the loss of horses. The *All Ireland Traveller Health Study* conducted in 2010 found suicide to be the cause of 11 percent of all Traveller deaths.[2] The male suicide rate among Travellers is seven times higher than among the general Irish population, and Ireland has one of the highest suicide rates in the world. Margaret McCarthy, who had lost three of her seven children to suicide, asked George to photograph the shrine she had built at Spring Lane in their memory. She told how her eighteen-year-old son, the most recent suicide, had hung himself with a belt from the ceiling of a shed and that no one knew why. She speculated he was still upset over the suicide of his sister the year before. Later that day, Jonathan, another of Margaret's sons, led George into a washhouse for a private chat. While sitting atop a washing machine, he described discovering his brother's body and then recalling the night before when his brother had told him, "I'll see you in the future." The comment struck Jonathan as odd, but he didn't connect it to an intention to commit suicide. Margaret's family tragedy conforms to the dominant pattern of Traveller suicide, in which most are committed by young males who take their lives by hanging, often following the death of someone close.

With virtually every Travelling family we visited, suicide reared its ugly head. On one occasion a scheduled filming was canceled after a suicide in the family. In several instances we discovered that our photographs from the 1970s included children who had later committed suicide. We met a young man at Holylands who'd never before seen a photograph of his sister Maggie, who had taken her life at age fifteen. On the verge of tears, he asked for the print, knowing his mother would cherish it. Suicide, thus, is not entirely new to Travellers. When we arrived at Holylands in 1971 a suicide had just occurred. But today they are far more common. A major study of Traveller suicide by social worker Mary Rose Walker concluded that the underlying causes are the breakdown of their former way of life, a loss of identity, and rejection by mainstream society.[3]

Margaret McCarthy in front of the shrine she built in memory of three of her children who had committed suicide, 2011.

As our journey proceeded, we visited homes where Mass cards commemorating family members who had died were taken off the fireplace mantle and handed to us and the tragic story of each death told. It was difficult to know what to say, especially as people typically relive the pain as they relate the circumstances of what happened. Jim Connors believes that many suicides are due to Travelling men's reluctance or inability to express their feelings, which then build to a point where suicide seems like the only option.

> Travelling People, they just commit suicide, and if you catch them and you cut them down, they'll go back and do it again. They keep on doing it and keep on doing it until they succeed. Mind you, I've thought about it meself from time to time but I always got over it, got over that hurting. . . . A lot of Travelling people are very private people. They don't like talking. It could be money problems, it could be father and mother problems, and a lot of problems are created in their own head. When they get something bad, a bad feeling, they can't express their feelings. . . . It just explodes then. Awful arguments results. Could be deaths that results. Could be a court case that results. Once you get a bad feeling, you're going to take it out on something or somebody. . . . Damage yourself, damage your property, or damage something else. That's the only way you're going to express that feeling. End of story.

When living at Holylands in the 1970s, we came to believe that one of the greatest hardships that illiteracy and the lack of formal education imposed on Travellers centered on communication. Without the words to label or to fully express their thoughts and feelings, frustration built up, often erupting in violence, especially when people had been drinking. Men were also expected to be tough, and all Travellers are rather stoic, which makes expressing feelings or doubts—anything that might be interpreted as weakness—difficult. One result, as Jim Connors said, is to "damage yourself, damage your property, or damage something else." Moreover, when the vocabulary to label a phenomenon like "discrimination" does not exist, it is perceived as individual experience and kept private, and the pain it causes grows unabated.

5

KATHLEEN MONGAN KEENAN
Pushed from Pillar to Post

Kathleen Keenan is a soft-spoken and attractive women in her fifties, the mother of three boys and seven girls. She was born on the road but now lives in Meelagh View, one of Mahon's two group housing schemes for Travellers. Outside her house is a shrine to the Virgin Mary, built by the Cork City Council. Kathleen's story provides a personal account of life on the road and the uneasy transition to settled life. She also offers a middle-aged Travelling woman's perspective on various aspects of culture change.

I WAS BORN IN A TENT IN THE MIDLANDS IN BIRR, COUNTY OFFALY. IT WAS 1958 on the fifteenth of March. At that time Travelling women weren't checked by doctors—there was no doctors coming to you on the side of the road back in the '50s and '60s. My mom was only after having me when she sent my two sisters up to a farmer's house to get some milk. I had a little sister eight years old and an older sister, Maggie. So they went and asked the farmer for milk, and my little sister asked for a drink of water. The farmer gave her the drink of water, and when he did, she just fell at Maggie's feet. She died. It was her heart. My mother was just after giving birth to me in the camp. God sent one and took the other.

My mother had a family of fifteen. Nine died, and she ended up with six living. There was a lot of babies born blue. She probably needed a C-section for some of them, but she never went to no clinics. There was no doctors, no scans, no iron tablets, nothing. She'd become pregnant, and that would be it. She'd wait the nine months to get the labor pains and call one of the Travelling women to be there with her. I think she only had two born in hospital. Myself and my older brother and sisters were all born in the camp with only Travelling

A smoky glimpse of family life in a
shelter tent in county Mayo, 1972.

Kathleen Keenan holds a restored version of a photograph taken of her in 1968 by actor Robert Mitchum, who was in Ireland filming *Ryan's Daughter*, 2011.

women to help. When my father knew my mother was going to have the baby, he'd be up on the bicycle or in the pony and car [cart] looking for a nurse. The nurse would come out afterwards to see was the afterbirth out and was the baby all right. The Travelling women would have everything done. They burned the afterbirth to keep away the sickness and bad luck from the child and burned the sheet or anything that had blood on it. Sometimes a child was born with a lucky cap—that was a veil of skin over their head. Nearly all of the mothers at that time would keep that because it was very lucky and would give other women bits of it for curing. There's a lot of young women now forgetting the old *pishogues*. We call them *pishogues,* but the settled people call them old wives' tales.

I lived in a tent for years and then a wagon. My father did tinsmithing—pots and pans, all of that. And he would make wagons and cars [carts]. And he would help out farmers if they wanted anything done, say, spuds. We never lived around cities. The biggest town that we knew was Listowel in the county Kerry. It was in Listowel where my father first drew the dole. He was working for the town on the roads with a couple other Travellers, and I don't think they had any more work for him. He heard about the dole and signed on and got paid for my mother and ourselves. This photograph here was taken in Listowel back in 1968 or '69.

The land was belonging to a solicitor named Pierse. He was a very good-hearted person. We pulled in outside his gate. It was lovely, really lovely with grass and trees, but it was on the main road going from Listowel to the Tarbet ferry, and it was very, very busy. Robert Mitchum, the actor, took this photo (page 73). He was working on *Ryan's Daughter,* and one day he came in a nice big car and pulled in outside the gate. He had a cameraman with him, and he just came in and shook hands with my father and asked about the family. And my father explained the whole lot to him, and he was amazed. He asked my father did we live in a caravan and tent all our life. My father explained that we did and that he was born in a camp himself, and that my mother was born in a camp, and that nearly all the family was. Robert Mitchum took a lot of photos and asked my father if he would let myself, my two brothers, and my two sisters act [as extras] in the film. My father was all for it at first, but then he heard that we would have to stay overnight [outside his supervision]. "No way," he says, "no way. Not a hope in hell." So that was the end of our film career.

After we'd been there awhile, Mr. Pierse came down one day and said to my father that if he wanted, we could move into his land for free. We wouldn't have to pay rent or nothing and it would be safe for the children and there was loads of acres and water that we could use for the horses. "You can stay in there as long as you like," he says. My father was delighted, of course, and agreed because we'd been getting pushed from pillar to post, and my mother had put us to school. My sister Maggie was working in a factory just below us. Then Mr. Pierse got the Corporation [city council] to give us a mobile home, but we still had our wagon and our car [cart]. This mobile home was like a palace to us because we were used to only the tent and the wagon. Mr. Pierse built us a lovely kitchen, and beside it was a toilet and shower. It was beautiful.

Then the tragedy happened. I was about eleven and had made my confirmation and first Holy Communion. My father and mother went down to Birr one day to see my grandfather. He was an old soldier. He'd fought in the 1914 war, and he was living in the barracks in Crinkill. He was very old, so my auntie asked if my sister Maggie could go down and help—bring him in and out to the toilet, in and out to bed, and help with the washing and

A young girl rests inside her family's cozy winter shelter built from scrap lumber collected at a landfill, 1971.

all that. My father and mother said, "Of course." So my sister went down and was playing outside in the evening, kicking a ball around with the boys and girls. She was leaning over to kick the ball and another fella was going to kick the ball and he gave her an awful kick in the left part of her chest. She died instantly.

The doctors were telling my mother that she probably strained a muscle and could have had a heart problem. That was the last time I ever saw my sister Maggie. We left Listowel then, after the death, and moved away down to Ennis, county Clare. My father got into drinking then over my sister being dead. He sold the ponies and he sold our caravan, and we ended up on what was called the Old Dump Road. He made a hut out of timber for us. It was a very sad time. A few months later we got a mobile home on a halting site. We were there for about a year, and then we got a house up in Clarecastle in Ennis, county Clare. Both my parents died there in Clarecastle.

Ennis made sites for all the Traveller families. They have one site for the Mongans and another site for the McDonaghs. There was a training center in Ennis too [St. Joseph's Education Centre]. Sister Margaret McFadden—she was from the North—introduced us to Paddy Houlahan. We all had school, and he came along and opened up this training center in an old convent place. We used to get a fiver a week for going. This five pound, now, was like gold to us because we never had any pocket money. Paddy was learning us songs and loads of bits and pieces. He was a great fella. He used to bring us away on trips and hikes up there in Pat Galvin's farm. We climbed the Reek. There was a place in Ennis open for tourists that had bikes for hire, and he used to hire out the bikes and we used to go out to Dromoland Castle. It was very, very old and broken down at the time, but we used to go out there and have picnics. He was very, very good. He wrote a very good song about Travellers, "In the Dark." Did you ever hear it?

I got married in 1977 and moved onto the road again. I was just eighteen. I was delighted to move back onto the road. We moved to Dublin, myself and John. We had a tent for the first year and a half and we were proud of it, because that's all we had. Then we got a wagon. Then we sold the wagon and we got a trailer. We were moving up.

I had eleven children and have ten living: three boys and seven girls. My youngest is now fifteen. I buried my oldest girl. She died when she was three. We were traveling in Wales, and she was with my two nephews, my brother Mark's sons Martin and Jim. They were out playing and they picked up some tablets. People was after throwing away rubbish where we camped. They were red depression pills, but they looked like Smarties so the children ate them. The two boys didn't eat as much and vomited some up. But she swallowed them, God love her. I brought her to the hospital, but they went to her brain too quick.

I was in England myself a long time after getting married, and I loved it. The place I loved the most was around Northampton because when my father and mother were alive, we were all over there together. There was about twenty or thirty families from Ireland over there. All my cousins and my husband's cousins were there. There was this big field and no gate. It was just open, so we all moved into it, and we were just left there as long as we kept the field clean.

We used to get all the rubbish and burn it in a big bundle. That was in the '80s. We lived in a trailer and moved around for years until we came to the old halting site here in Cork. It was wrecked and kind of run-down, but there are so many happy memories about that old site. Travellers camped there for years. They moved in and back out, then back in. The men were happy there. They played horseshoes, pitching, and tossing. They'd all mix and go out for a chat. We were happy there. But since we moved into Meelagh View and into Meelagh Drive [joint group housing schemes], we're not mixing as much.

How did Meelagh come about?

Well, our social worker Maureen—she's from the Corporation—asked what we'd like if we were going to get a place. We said we'd like a place away on our own. The O'Reillys said the same. Maggie [O'Reilly] had too many small children, and the boys had so many horses that we couldn't be too near together. We couldn't fit. Then one morning Maureen rang and said that we were getting our own places and to come down and pick areas, so we did. We picked areas, and the O'Reillys picked areas. But we never got those areas. We were all put here in the one place. And, as you can see, there is only a ten-foot wall between both families, and there is a lot of horses and there is a lot of children as well.

We have no problem with the O'Reillys. And the O'Reillys have no problem with us. It's just that there's too many families here. In our family, one son has six children, the other one has three children, and the other one has four children. I went into the Corporation myself, and my sister and my aunt Julie and my husband went in a lot of times and told them we didn't want to go into the site because we didn't want it built here. We wanted it built a bit further down, but they said, "No." We says, "Then we aren't going into it." They said, "If we are offering you accommodation and you don't want it, then just pack your bags and go away with you. There is nothing else we can do for you." We didn't understand the layout of the houses either. They were showing us this map [blueprint], but we didn't understand the map because it was only all lines up and down. They were explaining to us, "This is the bathroom. This is the kitchen. And this is the living room. And this is your backyard." But we couldn't make out what it was, so we asked them to do a matchbox model for us, but they never did.

When we were down at the old site, my husband bought this big container. He made a training thing [gym] in it much like the one Francis Barrett [the Olympic boxer] had. He got boxing bags and gloves for the boys. When we were moving into the site, I said we weren't going without the container. I wanted it in the backyard. But the Corporation said, "No, we'll sort you out. We're giving you a big room in the community center." You saw that big

Boys work out in one of the many small gyms Travellers have created in shipping containers and sheds, 2011.

room over there? It was supposed to be a training center for the boys. The shower was put in there for them and the toilet. The Corporation said they'd support it, and I said I'll keep it clean and tidy. They said they'd give us the electric free, but that never happened. They wouldn't even give us a key to the community center. Even if we wanted to have a Christmas party for the children, it was, "No."

My husband never wanted to come into the house. He never wanted group housing. But I wanted to try out the house, so I kept at my husband. He finally gave in, and we moved in. I don't think we were six months in the house when my husband got badly depressed. He was so confined, you see; he was so confined in the house. He wouldn't hardly talk at all. He wouldn't mix. He'd just go into the living room and keep looking at the television. And his appetite went. I knew there was something wrong. His face was drawn, and he kept saying, "I can't live like this. I just can't live like this—just like a prisoner. I have to move back outside to the road. I have to get out of here. If I don't get out of here, I'm going to die." So we did.

We got up one morning and went and bought two old trailers. We had a van at the time, and we decided we would pull out to the Mallow Road. We had a lovely little spot not far out of the city, and we were very happy—just myself and my husband and my daughter Kathleen. She moved out of her house as well with her husband and her children. I put the children going to school in Blarney, which was close to our camp. They loved it; they really did. They felt at home with all the children there. It was great. My husband could go up the land we were staying on and see the ponies and trot his ponies and go around hunting with the dogs in the evening. He'd have a big fire lit outside, a sup of tea, and a chat. You can't have that in a house. If you light a fire out here, the fire brigade is out on top of you. So that's a big part that's gone now from the men's life. But then, of course, they [city council employees] came on and said that we'd have to move back into the house. We weren't getting left on the road. It was a very sad day when we were leaving the Mallow Road to come back in again. My husband just went down to the pub and got drunk. He couldn't take it. He's not as bad today, but he still does not like the house.

Even myself, I have this big hunger, this big urge inside me to just get back up and go live on the side of the road. I'd love to go out in a tent or a wagon again for the summer. My own sons and daughters go away every year to England. My two girls have been at me all summer, "Get up and go. Get up and go." But I'm still working in the community center with the children. But hopefully the end of July or August we can go. But if I get my husband a trailer and bring him on the road, he mightn't come back.

My family couldn't stick being on the site the whole year round. No way. They stay here in the winter all right, with the children going to school, but as soon as June or May comes, they take the children out of school and go on away over to England. They won't come back until September for school. The ones that have no children in school, they won't come back until about November. I have grandchildren in England now. They get on the phone to me, and I ask them, "How do you like it over there?" And they say, "Oh Mammy, we love it. Come on over. It's lovely because we're going around and seeing other people and seeing other places."

The house affects the men worse than the women. Women have more space for the children, and there are toilets and electricity. And we have the washing machine and the drying machine. Even the children have gotten used to having the house; they wouldn't like to be on the road in the wintertime. And the women are always busy, doing all sorts of bits and pieces. But there's not much work for men to do now. There isn't many things to occupy their mind—no old fire lighting outside, no cup of tea and a chat, no game of cards, no tossing or pitching or playing horseshoes. They don't do that anymore. They stick in the house; they're there all the time. The men don't want to let go of the old times—the old times is locked in their system.

My husband now tries to get away. He's gone now with a friend of his named Tom. He's a settled person, actually, but he's been with Travellers for years and years. He is my husband's best friend. They go away every second day out the country about twenty or thirty miles away. They go the back roads with their flask of tea and go away trotting with their two horses. Sometimes they'll park the car and bring the dogs up in the field and hunt. Some of the younger guys—the ones that go through education, learn to read and write—are different. They can do other things, and they're more used to the city. You have to change as the world goes around; of course you do.

I've been volunteering for years. I'm a tutor at our center. I help the children to read and write, and I'm there if one of the children kicks up with a settled person or any of the other tutors. I am there to control them. They look up to me. I am like a matriarch to them. They won't carry on or misbehave when I'm there. It's good to have an older Travelling person around working with the younger Travellers. The first place I ever went to talk to settled people about Travellers was St. John's College. The first questions they ask me is, How are we coping with the houses? Do we miss our old way on the roadside? How are we getting on with the community? Are we still as proud to be a Traveller? How are the children settling into school? Would we ever like to go back on the road again? I tell them how we feel.

What other changes are happening in Travellers' lives?

Young girls don't have big families no more. They're getting this thing in their arm, the injection, and more of them is getting the patch. There is more help for women now and more information about birth control. We have groups in Cork—Travelling women's groups and settled people as well—that come around and explain the whole story to women or go with them, if they're too shy, into the family planning clinic. My mother, my aunties, and all the older women did not believe in anything that would interfere with God's will because they'd be afraid that when their daughters were grown, God wouldn't send them any children. It was God's will if they had a child every nine months. My mother had them nearly every year. She never complained—never complained, she didn't. I was born with a dislocated hip, but the old people wouldn't bring you to get anything done with it and you weren't checked up. It was their belief that God willed that. They would be afraid that if you interfered with God's work, you could end up not walking at all or in a wheelchair. So that's why I ended up with my limp. That's why most of the poor women died young as well. We've come a long, long way.

There are women here who could never read or write but can now because they went back to school. A good lot of us now can read and write—not perfect, but we can do it. The women are doing it more than the men. Marriage is changing too. There is a lot of marrying cousins. My son James married his first cousin, his aunt's daughter Julia. My daughter married a far-off cousin, Bernie McDonagh. My daughter Lisa married another cousin; he's a McDonagh too. My son Martin, he's a boxer, married Lisa's husband's sister. So they had a double wedding: brother and sister married brother and sister. Today it seems some are getting married younger—way younger, way younger. It's amazing. I would rather girls be around the eighteen mark. Then there is some girls today that do not want to get married and have kids. I have another daughter now, and she's around eighteen and has no intention of getting married. She does not want to get married. No way in the world.

Things just keep changing and changing. Maybe even ten years ago there were still match weddings [arranged marriages], but a lot of them didn't survive because the girl and the boy didn't know each other, had nothing in common. Some of them only lasted six, maybe twelve months. And there were some girls left pregnant or left with the baby and no father for it. Men, mostly, would get up and go away with somebody else, but the women would linger on to see if the husband would come back and give it another go for the sake of the child or because she was pregnant. I never matched anyone for any of my family. I'd rather for my children to get up and talk to a boy or a girl for a while before they get married. They should know what they're getting into and if they have anything in common. There were some weddings before where the boy wouldn't even see the girl and the girl wouldn't see the boy. The match came up through drink, between the men [fathers]. The mothers would say, "Ah, look, don't be coming out with that kind of talk." But the men would want it. Some children were only thirteen years of age, for God's sake, and then they'd be getting married at fifteen or sixteen. A lot of those marriages didn't work out.

In the old days we had open weddings, you know, outside. We'd have a few cases of Guinness or cider, a big cake, and sandwiches. I remember my mother telling me that when she got married, the Lord have mercy on her, all the women went off to the houses begging, and they got a load of pigs' heads and spuds and cabbages. They had five big fires, and they boiled about fifty or sixty cabbage heads with the pigs' heads in huge pots. The salt off of them probably was ridiculous, because they were all home-cured heads at that time. And that was your wedding dinner. An awful lot of farmers would come down, eat that dinner, and sit down and drink Guinness with them.

But the girls now, they want their hotels. They want their Hummers and big cars and white dresses and their big cakes. The weddings are expensive now, but nothing like the Gypsy weddings. Now, I'm not a rich person. Even if I was a rich person and I had money, there is no way I would have a Gypsy wedding. Not a hope in hell, no way. Those poor young ones, they're completely punished with the weight of the dresses alone. One of them [on television] fell into the car. With my daughters I bought the clothes—the wedding dress and all. I bought the cakes, and I rented the Hummer. My daughter did have a Hummer. Then my husband, with the groom's father, got the hotel, the cameramen, and the music. The mother of the groom bought the groom's clothes and all that. The girls buy their own ring, and the boys buy theirs.

Travellers dress a lot different now. They wear more jewelry and more gold. And they cut their hair now. Before, you'd be killed. Travellers all loved the long hair—ponytails and plaits. You'd be afraid to comb your hair for fear you'd break it or something. And before, a girl wouldn't be allowed to drive a car. Now the girls have their own license and cars. Some of them have jobs, and some have passports.

There are also a lot of silly girls going away on holidays on their own, which would be one thing I would not allow. The most popular place for them is the Canary Islands; loads of them go there. It could be six girls get up together and go. I wouldn't allow my girls to go on a holiday on their own—only if me and my husband was with them. The only holiday I've ever been on was to Lourdes—it was lovely—I brought my daughters with me. Now, some Travellers are traveling over to Spain and other foreign countries. Before, they would be afraid to get on a boat and be afraid of their life to get on a plane. My husband is still afraid to get on a plane. I was very nervous myself, I must say, when I went to Lourdes. My daughters made a laugh of it. When Travellers go over to Spain and France, they can get scrap and other bits and pieces and rubbish jobs and make some money. Some of them go over for the summer months and come back in the winter to their houses. Some of them stay for years.

Now that most Travellers are living in houses, do they still consider themselves Travellers? Do their children?

None of my children and grandchildren—I think it's twenty-one grandchildren I have—will deny who they are. I have six grandchildren up in Newbridge. Four of them are in school, and my grandson gets into fights when the other children say, "Oh, you're a knacker and a tinker." Some of the children do discriminate against them. Not a lot, now, and I must say my grandson has very good friends who are settled children. He just says, "I am proud of who I am." My daughter was on to me yesterday, and she was telling me that where she lives there are a couple of people that don't like Travellers and there are a couple of children that put their nose up to them. So my grandchildren—one is eight and the other is nine—they go out and sit on the top of the wall and sing, "I was born a tinker." And that puts the settled people mad.

The families I know around here, they never hide that they are Travellers. I think that whoever hides that they are Travellers should be ashamed. You should never hide who you are. Even if you are a tramp walking on the road, don't ever hide who you are. But there are some Travelling women out there and some Travelling girls who do put on a settled person's accent—you know, a swanky kind of tone and big words. A lot of us don't know the big words yet. If there is a meeting going on with both Travellers and settled people being there, some Travellers won't hardly even look at another Travelling person—they kind of move away. But they know. Deep down they know that they are Travellers. It really annoys me. I think it's so stupid. Really, I pity them. We are proud of our name, of who we are, and where we come from.

6

THE ROAD TO ENNIS

L EAVING CORK WE HEADED NORTHWEST, WITH ENNIS, COUNTY CLARE, AS our destination. We had two days off before our next rendezvous with the film crew and decided to stop along the way. We visited Killorglin first, the small market town where George had taken some of his earliest photographs of Travellers. It is best known as the site of Puck Fair, an ancient horse and cattle market during which a wild goat is captured, crowned, and tethered atop a forty-foot platform in the town square to preside as "King Puck" over the annual three-day gathering. It is also a place where Travelling People come to sell horses, renew ties with far-flung kin, and, in earlier years, arrange marriages—which was especially fitting since the puck (male goat) is a pre-Christian symbol of fertility. Lots of drinking also takes place, contributing to bloody "faction fights" between rival Travelling families in years past.

Although it was too early for the mid-August event, Killorglin looked much as it had in 1971 with colorful two- and three-story slate-roofed buildings lining its hilly streets, their narrow shop-front signs announcing family establishments: Sheehan's Lounge, Cahillane Butchers, Quinlan's Kerry Fish, and O'Grady's Bar. Just being in the town again brought back memories. We had left Dublin just a few weeks into our research to travel to Puck Fair, knowing that fairs were important places where Travellers gathered. Once there, we had dodged animals, buskers, revelers, and tourists to make our way to the hodgepodge of caravans, wagons, and Ford Escort vans that made up their camp on the edge of town. Here we had wandered around attempting to talk to people. Most Travellers had been cordial enough, but we were strangers on their turf, and they were at the fair to have fun, which didn't include answering the questions of two young Americans. Walking away from one group, a cheeky teenager had thrown a clod of horse dung at us.

From Killorglin we drove on to Fenit, where I had spent my first summer in Ireland forty years earlier as one of ten graduate students in a cultural anthropology field school. To discourage visiting each other and to promote our immersion into local culture, the program's director had scattered us in villages across Ireland. In this era before cell phones, Internet, and e-mail, we were unable to communicate with each other, and most of us didn't even know where the others were located. It was a lonely summer. After spending my first few nights in what I now remember as a cot in a broom closet in Godfrey's Hotel—no other room had been available—I found a place to stay in Carty's Bed & Breakfast. Mr. Carty was a *garda* stationed in Kenmare; his wife, Theresa, ran the

A mother finishes her morning grooming at Puck Fair, county Kerry, 1971.

small family business. Despite their kindness, the household had an air of sadness about it—their only child had died a few years before.

Now, George and I walked up and down Fenit's main street twice before recognizing their remodeled house; sadly, the Cartys had since died. Other aspects of Fenit have also changed. The commercial fishing crews that once gave me the crabs they inadvertently caught in pots set for lobsters destined for France are gone, replaced by recreational fishers. The town now has a new marina built with EU money, an active sailing club, and an imposing bronze statue of St. Brendan the Navigator, the fifth-century cleric who is said to have crossed the Atlantic before Columbus. These, together with annual events like its Christmas Day swim, mark sleepy Fenit's reawakening and transformation into a coastal tourism center.

The next morning we set out for Ennis, driving through Rathkeale, a small county Limerick town (pop. 1,550) with a strong association with Travellers. During our fieldwork, it already had a unique reputation as the place where a number of Travellers had built and owned large houses at a time when most families lived in modest caravans and wagons parked on the roadside or on newly built government sites. Before their cityward migration, most Travellers followed fairly restricted circuits within two or three counties; only some traveled widely, crossing the county and into the UK. These "long-distance Travellers," as they were referred to by local authorities and many settlement workers, often traveled in large groups, which made their arrival in a locale intimidating and problematic for the settled community. At the time, most dealt in antiques, laid tarmac (asphalt), or sold carpeting and other merchandise, but some were implicated in burglaries and the sale of stolen goods, particularly Georgian silver. Many of these families used Rathkeale as their home base.

Today 80 percent of the property in Rathkeale is said to be owned by Travellers. Most families are gone for ten months of the year pursuing entrepreneurial activities throughout Europe and living in caravans in campsites and trailer parks. When they return home to Rathkeale in November, they triple the town's population. Although we didn't know it as we drove through, the criminal elements of Rathkeale's Traveller population—dubbed the "Rathkeale Rovers" by international media, Europol, and other law enforcement—were then in the midst of a new criminal enterprise: ripping rhino heads off the walls of natural history museums and the trophy rooms of great houses and castles across Europe to sell at enormous profit to middlemen or directly to Chinese and Vietnamese clients who value powdered rhino horn for its reputed medicinal and aphrodisiac properties and, when mixed

Sharon listens as Pat Galvin describes the change in Traveller life in Ennis, county Clare, 2011.

with wine, as a new "emblem of conspicuous consumption."[1] Always identified in the media as Irish Travellers, this group and their scams and lawlessness tarnish the reputation of all Travellers and link nomadism with criminal behavior, further delegitimizing it as a valid way of life. Travellers recognize this and often identify "the Rathkealers"—referring to this criminal element—as a problem for the entire community.

Upon reaching Ennis that evening, we contacted Pat Galvin, who for many years was an active member of its Itinerant Settlement Committee. We first met Pat in 1971 and looked forward to seeing him. On the way to his house the next morning, we drove past a stretch of road along scenic Ballyalla Lake still lined with waist-high boulders placed there to prevent Travelling families from pulling in. No longer necessary because of legal restrictions against roadside camping, they remain as unsightly reminders of Ireland's opposition to the nomadic life Travellers once lived.

Greeting us at his farmhouse door, Pat was the same bespectacled bachelor with a lean frame and gentle demeanor I remembered. Retired from his job as a butcher and very recently from his volunteer work with Ennis's ISC, Pat poured us cups of tea and sat down to talk about his lifelong involvement with Travellers, or the *lucht siúil* ("walking people"), as many in his parents' generation had called them.

> *They used to come to our house for milk, hay, or anything we could afford to give them. My parents were very sympathetic. We were a family of ten, and our parents knew very well their own hardships and Travelling People's hardships. . . . When I was about seven, we had a big fire in the chimney of our old house. When we rushed outside, I could see the blaze coming out and hear the mighty roar. I remember thinking we were going to be out living in the road like the tinkers. It was a big shock, and I thought to myself if I can ever help the Travelling People, I'll do it. Twenty years later, the opportunity arose when I was invited to join a committee.*

Ennis was one of the earliest towns in Ireland to form a settlement committee, just four years after the 1963 publication of *The Report of the Commission on Itinerancy,* which launched the national movement. "It recommended assimilation," Pat explained, "and the provision of halting sites where Travelling People would be entitled to stay and, hopefully, be able to send their children to school. That was the thinking when we started to work here in Ennis."

The immediate impetus to settle Travellers, however, was to eliminate the problems they were creating for house dwellers. "The government wanted to solve the problem that was causing it headaches," Pat went on, "such as Travelling People staying in one place for a long time, their horses roaming around and trespassing on the farmers' land, and the neighbors all complaining. That was the real issue." But many settled people, including Pat, were primarily motivated by the report's descriptions of the dire conditions Travelling families lived under and the statistics on their high rate of illiteracy, infant mortality, and the like. "The settled people at the time were generally supportive of doing something to help," Pat remembered.

> *The first meeting I went to was in a big room in the hotel. People were busting out the door, so I couldn't go in very far. I was quite pleased by this [turnout]. They began to talk about the possibility of finding places for these "sites" that the government was willing to provide and how Travelling People could then send their children to school to learn to read and write. The problems arose later when we went to talk to the council: "Where were the sites going to be?," "Where was the land going to be found?," and all that stuff. And if a settlement committee member were to walk up the road and just look over a wall, the neighbor people would think, "They want*

A mother (identified as Julia Keenan) and her children on the Watery Road outside Ennis, county Clare, 1972.

to build a site here," and the next day they'd have formed a residents' association to protest about it. Helping Travellers was OK, but helping them onto sites near people was frightening [to locals]. We struggled with that for a long time.

During our early fieldwork, more than seventy local ISCs, made up entirely of volunteers, were working across Ireland to assist Travellers, following the recommendations of central government. Most subscribed to a charity model of social welfare and seldom consulted or involved Travellers in their work—not that doing so would have been easy. Most Travellers at the time were uncomfortable expressing their views to settled people and were reluctant to say anything that might be interpreted as speaking for others. They were also unfamiliar with much of the vocabulary being used. Few Travellers during our fieldwork, for example, knew what the word "itinerant" meant or what "settlement" entailed. Although the official "sites" that settlement workers described to them offered amenities like running water and electricity as well as an end to the forced and frequent roadside evictions families endured, few Travellers could know what it would actually be like to live on one: to pay rent and utility bills, no matter how modest, and to live in one place.

One of the places we had visited in 1971 with Pat and a local priest was the aptly named Watery Road—a long, dismal, and perpetually waterlogged lane just outside of town. They had taken us there to show us just how bad living conditions were for most Travelling families in the area. Indeed, one of the first tasks Ennis's ISC had undertaken had been to buy waterproof canvas covers for the families camped in makeshift tents and barrel-top wagons along the road's narrow verge. Not long after, the ISC built three two-family sites. "At first we had only sites with two families on each because locals were afraid of having more," Pat explained.

Then we found that two families wasn't ideal either, because one family could fall out with the other and leave and then the other would get lonely and leave as well. So the county council increased the size of sites to four families, later to six. After a while Travellers wanted proper houses on the sites, so the council started providing them. It was difficult work. Travellers can change their minds very suddenly. They would tell you they wanted a site at a certain place and that nothing else would do; then, not long after, they would decide something else, like they now wanted a house on its own to get away from troublemakers on the site.

In recent years a group housing scheme in Ennis had to be closed because of conflict among the Travelling families living there. Feuding is an ongoing problem within the Travelling community. "Travellers don't mix in together," a Traveller in Cork had told us. "When you have mixtures on a site, there will definitely be problems. When there is only related families—brothers or sisters or cousins—if they have a problem, they'll sort it out. But if they're not related, it just goes on and on. Then you have feuds." In the past, Travellers relied on moving to resolve conflict. We had observed this while living at Holylands, and I had periodically mapped the locations of families as they moved on and off the site or else repositioned their trailers, wagons, and tents to avoid families they were at odds with. By the end of the year, I could hold the stack of these little drawings in one hand and fan them with the thumb of my other and watch trailers, wagons, and tents dart around and disappear from the pages in a crude form of animation.

Settlement, however, makes avoiding or resolving conflict in this way impossible unless a family is willing to give up their house or their spot on an official site and risk not getting another. If they are unwilling or cannot leave for other reasons—a family member is ill, for example, or their children are attending school—physical violence may occur. With the availability of guns and the use of other weapons today, such conflict is much more serious. "That's something they are not coping very well with," Pat acknowledged. "Men are the ones responsible for the feuding. Forgiveness is hard for all of us, but although Travellers talk a lot about God, they don't talk to him in these situations. Anger builds up, and they handle it themselves with violence and revenge. They are bad at backing down. They have this mythical notion of being a tough guy, a dominant force—the 'King of the Travellers' sort of thing. Turn the other cheek is not in their thinking." A few months before our return, five members of the Joyce "clan" had assaulted a member of a rival family with machetes at Drumcliffe Cemetery as part of an ongoing feud. Since then, other feuds in Ennis have made the headlines. Unfortunately, because Travellers are a minority group whose members are all unfairly painted with the same brush, when such sensational incidents occur—no matter how few individuals are involved—the reputations of all Travellers are damaged, reinforcing prejudice and discrimination.

When central government ordered local authorities in the late 1990s to accommodate all remaining Travelling families, many at first tried to undercount the number of Travellers native to their area as a way of lessening the expense this responsibility imposed and reducing public opposition. Local authorities were also told to consult with Travellers when drawing up their accommodation plans. In some places this was implemented in a way characterized by one government worker I spoke with as "consultation with your ears closed." But other local authorities did their best. Ennis's volunteer ISC also had made a good-faith effort over the years to consult with Travellers. "All the Travelling People were interviewed and involved," Pat Galvin remembers.

It wasn't always easy. You have all types of attitudes. Travellers look for different things. Some want to live close to town, and others want land out in the country where they can have horses. Some want to be on a site, while others would like a place all their own. Some like the idea of living with settled people but having thefreedom to visit their relations elsewhere. It was difficult, and looking back we were probably too slow. Families would be waiting years and years for an improvement in their accommodation.

Today, more than six hundred Travellers live in Ennis—a large number for a town of 25,000. All are settled. Some live in public housing estates; others live in group housing schemes designed just for Travellers that accommodate six to twelve families. Ennis has no sites for mobile families, and when such families do show up in the area, even to temporarily sell merchandise from the roadside, they are moved on by the police. About 250 Roma from the Czech Republic and Slovakia now also live in Ennis, also in houses. As yet, we were told, members of the two groups have little to do with each other.

Ennis is also the site of Ireland's first training center for Travellers. St. Joseph's Education Centre opened in 1974 in a former orphanage before moving to new facilities some years later. The center taught literacy and vocational and craft skills like carpentry, welding, and sewing to fifteen- to twenty-five-year-olds. It became a popular social and recreation center, as Kathleen Keenan recounted in chapter 5, in large part due to the charisma of its first director, Paddy Houlahan, whose narrative makes up chapter 8. He injected fun into its education programs, encouraged self-expression, and believed in using sport and music to build confidence and pride in Traveller culture. With three young Travellers he formed a small band called the Wanderers and wrote, performed, and recorded songs with them. The lyrics of some, like "Campfire in the Dark," reveal a lot about many Travellers' longing for life on the road.

My father rises early and he makes a sup of tea
He lights the kitchen stove and then he calls me
His days are often empty, he's nothing much to do
So he sits and tells me stories of the travelling life he knew

In the evening they would meet in lonely country lanes
A field away you'd hear a collie bark
And they'd pass the time away with talks about the day
Standing 'round the campfire in the dark
Standing 'round the campfire in the dark

My mother likes the house, the hot water and the rooms
It's warm in the winter and she's handy with the broom
Sometimes she makes colcannon, more often griddle bread
There's a hunger deep inside her for a travelling life that's dead

In the evening she would lift the black pots from the coals
"A bit to eat" she always would remark
There'd be vessels left to clean while children could be seen
Playing 'round the campfire in the dark
Playing 'round the campfire in the dark

We'd go down to the pool hall and chat up the beors[2]
Sometimes at their discos we can't get past the doors
We're still tinkers to them and it's thrown at our ears
We're still the awful strangers after all these years

And I think about my own life and the way that it will be
An Escort van, a bit of dealing, a wife and family
Thursday I collect the dole, Friday pitch and toss
But on the site I think about the Travellers' ways we've lost

And I wish that I could rise, wash the sleep out of these eyes
And listen to the sweet song of the lark
And I wish I could be in that campfire company
With the sound of horses moving in the dark
With the sound of horses moving in the dark

Pat Galvin was active at St. Joseph's, too, which over time expanded its program to include Travellers of all ages. "From the earliest days, everything we did was aimed at education," he recalled.

When we started most of the youth didn't even know their letters. We were starting from scratch. Reading and writing just for the sake of reading and writing didn't mean much until the boys started going to the boxing club. Then everything changed. They wanted to read about what was happening in the championships and what was being said about them in the papers. Gradually they felt the need to read. The training center was great even for me. It made my life totally better. I didn't learn to swim until I was thirty-four, and I learned to swim with the Travelling People.

As adults began attending—one woman learned to read and write at seventy—they understood the value of literacy, which bolstered their commitment to their children's education.

When we returned in 2011, about thirty training centers for Travellers were operating across Ireland, although they were threatened with closure by the country's financial crisis. The following year they were gone, along with other Traveller educational services including resource teachers and visiting teachers. The government decided it could not afford to continue funding programs that produced what it regarded as minimal measurable returns. St. Joseph's now caters to all local welfare recipients, including Travellers, although at the time of writing no Travellers were attending.

Ennis's committee, like other ISCs around the country, never accomplished as much in Traveller employment. "Travelling People, especially the men, have never been very interested in ordinary sort of jobs like factory jobs," Pat told us.

> They have always wanted to be their own boss. They prefer to work at their own time and pace. Gathering scrap suited them very well. Another reason getting jobs has been difficult is that settled business people don't trust Travelling People. Some of this is because of rumors; some is because Travellers don't always make a good name for themselves. Settled people don't like being made the fool. Some Travelling People clean and fix slate roofs and do a good job, but others do a bad job and charge too much. The same goes for the tarmac [asphalt] people—the tarmac could be this thin [indicating half an inch]. If they do a decent job, people don't mind paying, but a bad job leaves a very bad taste. And today with so few jobs for settled people because of the crash, everything has slowed down. Even Travellers who would be out collecting scrap some time ago are now sitting at home because of the shattered economy.

While the employment rate for Travellers nationwide in 2011 was 16 percent, in Ennis it was said to be "practically nil" and for older men "nonexistent." About a dozen women were, however, training to become primary health care workers. In other parts of the country, too, small numbers of Travelling women hold mainstream jobs in shops, day care centers, and hospitals or with local government or Traveller organizations. Fewer Travelling men are employed, although some have become successful entrepreneurs, even in a bad economy.

Curious to see what the Watery Road looks like today, we returned there with the film crew and found a very different scene from the one recorded in George's early photographs. The road is now paved and lined with houses, including a cluster of six belonging to Travellers. Three of the semidetached units were well maintained, but the middle units were vacant with fire damage, boarded-up windows, and debris in their yards. I chose to approach the home with a lush lawn bordered by flowering shrubs, a front door flanked by cast concrete statues of a boy on a donkey and a boy with a horse, and cast-iron cooking pots, kettles, and a wagon wheel hanging from its boundary wall.

A young woman with yellow hair and black roots answered my knock and retreated quickly upon seeing me with George and the film crew just beyond. Soon her mother appeared, eyeing me warily as I explained our purpose and pulled out some photographs of the Watery Road in the 1970s. She examined them with interest, identifying some of the people in them—Mongans, Joyces, McDonaghs, and Keenans. Then, with the help of other family members who gradually emerged from the house, she tried to figure out from what vantage point each image had been taken—a challenge they all clearly enjoyed. I learned that Mary McDonagh Joyce had moved to Ennis from county Westmeath in 1980 and had been given a *tigín,* which was later replaced by the two-story semi-detached house before us. Two of her adult sons also live in houses on the road. Now in her late forties, she has nine children—another six had died—and twenty-five grandchildren.

As we talked, Mary's husband left the house, climbed into his van, and drove off without a word, reminding me of many other Travelling men who leave the business of interacting with outsiders to their wives. But, as I discovered later, John might have been eager to leave for another reason: he and his sons were the Travellers who had been charged with the assault of another Traveller at Drumcliffe Cemetery just a few months before. Finding two strangers and a film crew at the door was undoubtedly disconcerting.

Soon after John pulled away, another van pulled up. It belonged to a salesman from Canada representing the "Irish

Our Lady of Fatima waits in the Joyce family's living room on the Watery Road in Ennis, county Clare, 2011.

Society for Christian Civilisation" who was delivering a nearly life-size statue of Our Lady of Fatima. Mary had ordered it after finding a leaflet on her door and purchasing several of the "miracle medals" it advertised. Soon after, she received another leaflet describing the blessings Our Lady could bestow. As we talked, the salesman carried the statue into her living room, positioned it on the coffee table, and laid out pamphlets, pictures, and rosary beads. Mary was unclear about what would happen next. Speaking with the salesman later, I learned that the statue was on loan for a few hours only. The scene was a reminder of the superstitious nature of much Traveller religiosity—their belief in the power of curing priests, holy wells, and religious medals—and also of their vulnerability, since the loan of the statue was not free.

7
GALWAY

FROM ENNIS WE TRAVELED TO GALWAY CITY, WHERE IRISH CULTURE, literature, and language have long flourished. Today more than four out of five Travellers live in urban areas, with Galway ranking second after Dublin. We had made several trips there in the 1970s because of the city's large and more traditional Traveller population but also to learn more about the troubled relationship between them and the settled community. The word "rahoonery" had entered the national lexicon in 1969 to describe virulent anti-Traveller sentiment and action after residents of the Galway suburb of Rahoon turned violent while protesting the continued presence of a Traveller encampment in their neighborhood.[1]

The Galway we returned to differed dramatically from the provincial city we had previously known. In the 1970s it was common to see dozens of caravans, barrel-top wagons, and tents strung out along the roadside verges or clustered on wasteland on the outskirts of the city. George had photographed John Ward making tinware on the side of the road with the tools of his other trade—chimney sweeping—secured to the bicycle parked next to his barrel-top wagon. Later we met his imposing wife, Bridget, begging in Eyre Square wearing her signature black shawl, and I had used a few words of Gammon, momentarily stopping her in her tracks. Today, Galway's Travellers are no longer camped on the roadsides but live on sites and in houses.

While prejudice still exists, Galway has become more accepting of Travellers in part because they are no longer the only minority in town. Galway's population is now diverse with Poles, Latvians, Nigerians, and other immigrants walking its streets. Galway's campus of the National University of Ireland has also grown and internationalized. Students, many of them foreign, make up one-fifth of the city's population. The city also attracts a million tourists each year who come for the Galway Races and the many events in its rich arts and festivals calendar. Its lively pubs, which offer *craic* (Irish slang for "a good time") along with drink, appeal to residents and visitors alike.

That evening we rendezvoused with the film crew in a dimly lit pub with low ceilings and plenty of character to discuss whom we planned to see and possibilities for shooting in Galway. Mercifully, the cigarette smoke–filled haze that used to engulf us when we visited pubs with Travellers—smarting our eyes and saturating our clothes—was gone. Ireland had swiftly stubbed out smoking in all workplaces, including pubs, at the stroke of twelve one night in March 2004, introducing some of the toughest antismoking legislation in Europe. We decided to visit John Donoghue the next day at his home in Salthill, a former seaside resort but now a suburb of the city. John was one of Nan and Mick Donoghue's sons and Sally's eldest brother. He was one of my favorite people—smart, sensitive, and always good to talk to. We had kept in touch periodically by mail, usually holiday greetings, but hadn't actually seen each other in forty years.

After many wrong turns and several corrective phone calls, our three-car caravan arrived at the quiet cul-de-sac where John's house was located. Nothing about the house indicated that a Traveller lived there, but it did differ from the rest. Instead of curtains, a large cloth portrait of a Plains Indian superimposed on an American flag hung in the window, along with a spirit catcher and other New Age paraphernalia—not unlike an American college dorm room in the 1960s. Like his sister Sally and an unknown number of other Travelling children, John had been taken from his parents by the "cruelty men" (officers from the Society for the Prevention of Cruelty to Children, now the Irish Society) and placed in care as a child. Together with his brothers Joe and Willie, he'd been sent to St. Joseph's Industrial School in Letterfrack about fifty miles outside the city. Sally and their sister Mary had been sent to another Galway institution. In recent years, the mental, physical, and sexual abuses that took place at Letterfrack and other church-run institutions have been well publicized, shocking and angering the nation, but in the 1970s they were still hidden.[2] When John turned sixteen, he was released and went to work for a local farmer in exchange for room and board and a minimal wage. His brother Willie also became a "home boy," as the released teenage laborers were known.

Not long after I had published their mother Nan's life story in 1986, I received an overseas phone call from a middle-aged Irishman who refused to identify himself but wanted to tell me that the next book I wrote should be about home boys—the first time I'd heard the term. There was something haunting about his voice and the way he urged me to do so. After the abuse scandal broke, I better understood his call. John eventually made his way to Dublin, where he rejoined his parents and lived at Holylands during our research. Both he and Sally had frequently referred to their experiences, mainly to voice their general loathing of the Catholic sisters and brothers who had abused them and of the church in general, but they had seldom gone into much detail. Several years after we left Ireland, John married Teresa, a slight and emotionally fragile young settled woman who had been raised in an orphanage.

John met us at the door wearing a smile and a dapper navy blue suit. He would be giving away his niece at her wedding a few hours later. He welcomed us in, film crew and all, and explained that Teresa was on a pilgrimage to Knock.[3] They had been homeless for several years, and during our visit John related in gritty detail what it had been like living rough on the streets of Galway City. His brother Kevin had run into him once, barely recognizing him. Being homeless had taken a toll, evident in John's deeply weathered face, husky voice, congested cough, and worsened limp. Unlike the other Traveller homes we visited, John's was a shambles on the inside, yet he proudly led us through the kitchen and into the small backyard to show us the gazebo he was building. In this, he reminded me so much of his mother, warm and open and always working on some improvement project. When we returned to his tiny living room to talk, I noticed that many of the photographs we'd sent him over the years adorned the walls, including a large collage he'd assembled, similar to Sally's.

John gave a powerful on-camera interview in which he talked about his past and his bitterness toward Irish society and its neglect of both Travellers and institutionalized children. "The children in the school were basically poor or illegitimate," John began.

> I think the fact that we were Travellers [he, Willie, and Joe] made the brothers who ran it afraid of us, especially when we got a bit older and we weren't going to take shit from them anymore. In a way being a Traveller was a bit of safety, but only if your parents came to visit. The other kids who never had parents come around were very vulnerable and afraid. They had no one, and I used to pity them. The brothers told us we were lucky because we got three meals a day, but we were abused and I didn't see no luck in that.
>
> Some of the brothers live in Galway today, but we're not supposed to go near them. Maybe they think we're going to harm them, and I would if I could. One of them is married now and has got kids of his own and works in the church in town. I'm afraid to go in there because I know I'd just lose me head. The church makes out like he is a good citizen. After what he done to kids, it's fucking unbelievable.

Anthony Maughan rests on our trip in county Wicklow while our mare, Franny, looks on, 1972.

John also recalled some of his time working for the farmer who took him into "custody" after he was released from St. Joseph's at sixteen.

One day when the farmer went off to get his dinner, me and another lad were left there to carry on working, bringing in the hay—and we started messing, throwing hay at each other. We were only kids. Well, when he came back and heard us messing about, he got his pitchfork and hit me full force on the back. I just collapsed on the ground. But he wouldn't bring me to hospital. A nurse at the infirmary looked at me, and I was put to bed with a hot water bottle for months. I couldn't get out of the bed to go to the toilet or anything. The nurse had to do everything for me. The bastard wouldn't let me go to hospital to get proper treatment for it, and ever since that I've had trouble with me back and I think it stunted me growth.

John spent a long time poring over our photographs. A picture of the horses everyone had kept at Holylands prompted the following response:

Back then [1970s] you were allowed to have your animals around the sites. Today you're not. . . . They put you [Travellers] behind these big walls where you are not allowed to live your life the way you want to, the way you were raised to. They've pushed us off the road and taken everything away. And now they have ads on television telling people in Britain and America, "Come visit Ireland." And you see a wagon with a tourist in it going on down the road. Everything's now all geared for tourism. It's OK for tourists to travel on the roads but not us who was born, bred, and raised there. They've taken away our traveling way of life, but it's OK for them tourism companies to rent out horses and wagons and make money from it. The government tells us that we're not allowed to have a caravan around unless it's put on a site. What good it that? It's like having a bicycle that you're not allowed to ride. That's what they've done. They're taking our ways, and now they're making money out of it. Oh, this is Ireland.

When we asked John what he thought the value of our old photographs might be for young Travellers today, he responded, "They are very important to the new generation because they let people look back and see how it was back then. People can then calculate whether Traveller life is better or worse today. The pictures take us back to our roots, and we all should go back to our roots at some stage. I think there's more in the pictures than Travellers could say because of our lack of ways of describing things."

The film crew got a taste of the hostility that still exists toward Travellers in some quarters when they went outside to shoot the exterior of John's house and a portion of the street. Two neighbors emerged to object, saying they did not want their street identified on television with Travellers. "When I moved into the house here," said John, "I got a few threatening letters from people in the neighborhood":

"Get out. We don't want your kind here. Go back to where you come from." And all that. I showed the letters to the guards, but they said they had no idea who was doing it, and, "Until this person comes up and threatens you,

there's nothing we can do." But I had a good idea who had sent them, and I went down one night to the man's house at the end of the street and said, "We've got to sort this out." He was afraid to come out. His wife was shouting, "I'm calling the guards." I said, "Go on, call them. I've the letters that you sent." When they heard that, they didn't call the guards, and they wouldn't come out. The funny thing about it, a couple years later he got a job working at the Travelling community center out in Ballybane.

As soon as the crew finished outside, we left, giving John a lift to the city center and making plans to meet again in Dublin. Back in our hotel room, we phoned Paddy Houlahan and arranged to meet the next day. His narrative forms the next chapter.

8

PADDY HOULAHAN

Living on the Edge of Your Town

Wearing a leather jacket and his trademark faded blue jeans, Paddy cycled up to meet us outside his small Galway City flat, still radiating the youthful energy and enthusiasm for life we remembered from the 1970s. At that time Paddy was becoming well known in Ireland for his enlightened work with Traveller youth in Ennis and for the music his band of young Travellers produced. Now living in Galway, he continues to work with Traveller songwriters and musicians, also writing and recording his own music. He remains active in youth work and sports, although his clientele now includes new emigrants from Africa as well as Travellers. As we sat amid his musical instruments and stacks of books talking about his work and how circumstances have changed, Paddy often recited song lyrics that captured the essence of the topic.

THE WAY I STARTED WORKING WITH TRAVELLERS WAS COMPLETELY accidental. My sister Emma lived in county Clare, where her husband worked at a bank, and I went down in the Christmas of '73 to see them. Coming through Ennis, there was a poor shelter tent at the top of the Watery Road. It affected me, and I later wrote a poem about seeing it at Christmas.

While visiting my sister, a local priest, Father Crosby, asked me to come with him to see someone at the hospital. Afterwards he said, "We'll call in at these wee nuns for a cup of tea." So we called in and passed the time with them. About two weeks later I got this envelope asking me if I'd like to be involved in setting up a training center for young Travellers. I didn't know anything about Travellers, but I was looking for a purpose in life. I wanted

Travelling children living in poverty in a shelter tent on the Watery Road outside Ennis, county Clare, 1972.

to feel that I was needed some place, that I could do something. My mother said to me, as mothers do, "Get a pair of trousers and go down and see what they want." At the time it was all blue jeans for me, no trousers. Happily, it turned out to be the kind of job that I could stay in the blue jeans.

When I went down to meet them, there'd been a storm and flooding on the Watery Road, and a lot of the people had moved into the community center. They asked me would I stay over there with them. So I did. I had the guitar with me and I knew a couple of Elvis songs, and the Travellers were very friendly. At the time they were living in different conditions. There were some in *tigín* sites—small four-unit sites. There were some on the side of the road, some living in wooden huts and shelter tents. And there was one family in a local authority house. There were a lot of young Travellers in Ennis, and they didn't have any employment. Many of them didn't have reading or writing skills. So something was needed. The Sisters of Mercy give us this old orphanage for the training center. It was quite small, but it had a little courtyard that became a place for handball. I think the best part was that we did everything together—the Travellers and me. We had to renovate the place and paint it. We shared bowls of soup, bits of bread. It was very friendly. The center was a blank slate. People really didn't know what was needed. I decided that because of the Travellers' tradition in metalwork and in carpentry that we'd have those as basic elements, and literacy as well. So we first developed these.

I have always been interested in people's stories. I often find them intensely dramatic and moving. If anyone starts talking to me about their life, I'm immediately all ears, I suppose like you anthropologists. Anyway, I had this old blackboard up in the center, and I had a map of Ireland on it. I said to the kids, "Can you write a little bit about where you've traveled in Ireland?" The areas were all quite close by. Some people were traveling in the barrel-top wagons, so they'd been maybe fifty or sixty miles away. But one lad by the name of Pat wrote this story about his father losing a horse in county Galway and going to look for it and coming across this Traveller called the King Ward. He was known as King Ward because he was handy with his fists. So Pat's father asked King Ward had he seen his horse, and Ward said, "No, fuck off." Then Pat's father and King Ward had a fight, and Pat's father beat him. So the story had that little bit of color. I thought, "Now, that's really interesting," and I got these old typewriters, and we started to type out these little stories. Some of them were just like telegrams; people could only put together a sentence. Other people wrote longer ones. Some mornings I would say to the kids, "Have any good dreams?" One girl

PADDY HOULAHAN
105

Paddy Houlahan in his Galway City flat, 2011.

used to dream a good bit, and one morning she came up with a dream that when typed out was one and a half pages. It was about being pushed into a match [arranged marriage] when she was in love with this other guy. So the Travellers were writing. And they could write "fuck" if they wanted to as long as they spelled it right.

After that came a book of sorts. We had a book where the kids could say what they wanted, and then another book that visitors could look at. We used to hide some of the more tricky language in the stories if visitors came in—we cleaned it up a bit. Then we brought out a real book called *Many Voices, One Community*. And outta that we made about five hundred pounds, and we bought some electric guitars and drums and microphones and that was the start of our rock and roll band. I had been teaching music as well—basically, guitar, banjo, and harmonica. Anyone who was interested played. Then some of the lads wanted to have a band. We called it the Wanderers, and it became kind of a Travellers' band. It was myself, Pat Sherlock, John McDonagh, and Tom McDonagh—just the four. We used to play at weddings and sometimes for national meetings, like the National Council for Travelling People and the National Association of Training Centres. It was a fantasy of mine to be in a rock and roll band.

Then we played at a buffer's [non-Traveller] wedding—it was the brother of a teacher in the center. Someone came up after and said, "You guys play very badly." Compared to other bands, we were pretty poor. So I went to the center and said, "Lads, we've got to write our own songs because we can't play other people's." Then there was this national competition for a folk group and a competition for an original song. So I said, "OK, we'll bang out a song." I'd never written songs, and I'd always been mystified at how people came up with melodies. So we brainstormed. I said, "It'll have to be about Travellers because no one else will have a song about Travellers." Then one of the lads said, "A Travelling family comes to town." OK. And that led to

A Travelling family comes to town
Harder these days to find a piece a ground
To lay the fire, pitch the tent,
Curse upon Travellers paying rent

Then there was a chorus:

Why don't they leave us in peace
Leave us alone
All we want is a place of our own

So the lads signed us on for the competition, and around the center the kids began singing, "Why don't they leave us in peace." It was just cobbled together around the table. I picked up the guitar at the end and put the tune onto it. I realized then that songs could be made about a lot of things. They grew organically. One of the first ones was for Travellers in Galway up at Rahoon after they were attacked. A few of us went to Rahoon the next day to see if there was anything we could do. Of course there wasn't, but a song came out of that. And then other songs came, like "Campfire in the Dark."

In the center we encouraged tinsmithing, and some adult Travellers began to make stuff and we marketed it to tourists in Bunratty Castle. Another whole thing was legal rights. This was about 1978. Travellers weren't being allowed into dances. There was one girl in particular, Katherine Sherlock. She'd never been at a dance before; she was refused on the grounds that she was a Traveller. So we decided that we'd make a test case, a constitutional test case, and we went forward with it. Combat Poverty said they'd fund it. The Irish Council for Civil Liberties was interested in helping, and we met with them on a number of occasions. It provoked a controversy. There was a lot of disagreement on the board of the center. Half of them were professional people like bankers, and one guy was a solicitor. They were connected to the establishment and didn't want the case going forward. So the Travellers and myself had to go on strike, and some on the board decided that I would no longer have the power to sign checks. It was very tense for six or nine months. The Combat Poverty people came down and held a big meeting. They said that they were backing us and they stood for the Travellers. So the case went ahead. Unfortunately, the woman solicitor from the Irish Council for Civil Liberties left after about a year. We got another solicitor but after about another year, we got a notice that all our documentation had been lost. Pretty pathetic! Thinking about it now, there was something peculiar about it—how do all your papers get lost?

Two Joyce girls sit with their uncle Mick Donoghue at his campfire at Holylands, 1971.

Later, with the National Council for Travelling People, I was one of a small group who met the attorney general and pressed for a change in the law, but all we got were tea and biscuits—very fine tea and biscuits. That was it. The change came later. Ten or fifteen years later the law was changed, and people couldn't be refused on the grounds of who they were, be it Travellers or be it women. The legal thing was important.

There's been a great growth of confidence. Some of the girls in Ennis in '74 were lovely, terrific people, but they'd be begging on the streets because that's what their people did. It was part of the family economy. But with the center in Ennis, the girls were able to come in and earn a small amount of money. That gave them a big growth in confidence. They were able to learn sewing machine skills and made their clothes at the center. For equality's sake, I insisted that the boys at the center cook two days a week. In 1974 that was a bit unusual, and of course the lads went, "What?" But it was great and everybody enjoyed it. And they made some pretty tasty dishes.

Travellers love sports. Even the girls played football [soccer] in the early days. We formed a handball club at the center and competed against settled people. We won a cup, which was a big thing. And then we had a soccer team that joined the soccer league. I remember in the first year when I was the manager we were being beat 18–nil, 16–nil, 15–1. The year after I left as manager, we started to win. Besides being a reflection of me as manager, I think Travellers were gaining confidence. Y'know—"We can play. We can compete. We have skills. We can write."

When I came to Ennis I didn't know people, and Travellers were very welcoming. I liked them, and they became friends. We'd go to the movies together. We'd play ball. We'd play a bit of music. I probably wouldn't have done music if it hadn't been for them. Just to be allowed into their lives, to be befriended by them—it was very important to me. Ennis was kind of like a love affair for me because there was so much. Morning to evening I was immersed in the variety: the housing, sites, legal rights, the music, the sport, sewing machines and metalworking, all this stuff. And the whole mutual respect thing was there.

What else did you gain personally from being with Travellers?

You anthropologists know about this. It's the whole thing about having insight into a culture: hearing what it was like for them, why they think the way they think, their experiences on the land with the farmers, tinsmithing and horse dealing. I just loved hearing all the stories—to be allowed into that. And I suppose, too, there was the whole mysterious thing of how in the end I became like a Traveller in terms of writing the songs. It wasn't intentional; it just happened. I remember one of the ones I wrote, "Living on the Edge of Your Town":

The books you read at school do not mention me
Because I am the invisible man in this country's history
But I knew the farmer, I traded him a mare
I picked his beet, I shaped his tins, and I was welcome there
No more call for my trade
Everything is plastic made
No more travelling around
And I'm living on the edge of your town

Of course, I wasn't living on the edge of anybody's town, but it just seemed to come out of me, kind of naturally. The center suited me because I could do a lot of things I loved doing, and I had empathy with Travellers. I could feel, kind of, what it was like for them.

I got on well with most. Over the years some have asked me, "Have you ever had a fight with a Traveller?" The answer is no, although I've been threatened: "What the fuck do you think yer doing?" or "Who the fuck do you think you are?" But generally I tended to keep it calm enough at the center. One thing I realized with Travellers was that it was important to be an extrovert. So I let go of myself a lot more so the kids at the center could really see me and hear me. I worked in Ennis for about thirteen years, and then I came up to Galway and I got involved in community work with Travellers in Hillside and Ballybane. We did a lot of drama there. The Travellers would improvise dialogue, which we used as starting points for discussion. I also wrote some songs, and then music came more and more into it.

I now work with African kids, too. I had this humongous project with Africans, some settled kids, and some Travellers. I wrote a song, "We Are One," and we recorded it. The African parents are very supportive of music; they want to buy the instruments and they want their kids to learn. They have a very positive energy. Quite often I'm coming back [home] on the bike and I'll be smiling to myself thinking about what this one or that one said. It's been grand, and I love being near the ocean here [in Galway City], but Ennis was pretty special.

That brings up another big change—all the new immigrant groups in Ireland.
How do Travellers and the African kids get along?

There's no prejudice. You hear that there is but there isn't, although there can be name calling. They talk and play music together. Nice things happen, but it can be a bit tricky. Some days I'll be holding my breath because when things go badly, Travellers don't hold

Residents objected to camps like this one located next to a public housing estate in Dublin in 1971 for a host of reasons, both real and exaggerated: unsightliness, sanitation, wandering animals, noise, the nuisance of frequent requests for water, and more.

For entertainment, Mary Browne poses her young son James with a cigarette and Guinness in their Holylands hut, 1972.

back—they'll say the worst things possible. It's happened to me. One time I was refereeing indoor soccer and I gave a penalty, and this Traveller guy disagreed. "You Chancery bastard," he yelled, and he picked up his mobile phone and fired it at me. It missed me by that much [indicates half an inch] and smashed into the wall behind me. In sports it's always like that with Travellers. Of course, they pay for it in the organized games, in the leagues. You just can't do that. And over the years they have learned to become more disciplined.

Take boxing. It's been great for Travellers. Some parents start kids that size [indicates three feet high] boxing. You'll see very young kids going down to the gym. Boxing takes skill and links in with the macho part of Traveller culture. It's been good because when you box, you learn to control the violence. Boxing was big among Travellers even when I arrived in Ennis in '74, and a lot of Travellers have been very successful at it, like Francis Barrett being in the Olympics.

This reminds me of a story. On a site up in Hillside, there're these skips [bins] for rubbish. Some of the Travellers would put their rubbish into the skip and some would throw it on the ground beside the skip, so there was always a bit of a problem. After Frank [Francis Barrett] came back from the Olympics, I was talking to this buffer and he was saying to me, "They ought to make Francis Barrett a community worker up there." His idea was that Frank would have respect and that he'd be able to say to people, "Look, sort that out." I tried to explain to him, "In reality what would happen is that Frank would say to someone, 'Look, you been putting that rubbish over there. You need to put it into the skip.' And they'd say, 'Who the fuck do you think you are, Frank?'" It didn't matter that Frank was an Olympic champion, because when he came home a couple of weeks later, someone attacked him and his father with a knife. A couple of Travellers cut him up. People have this idea that certain Travellers can just lay down the law, but that's not true. Even if you're strong and tough, the other guy will get four guys and come after you.

I've written a lot of songs for young Travellers, and Travellers are writing their own songs. Again, it's part of that confidence; "We can do it." There's a girl here, Bridget Mongan; she has a song called "The Everlasting Rose." She wrote a lot of it on her own. There was a small room in the community center up in Ballybane for music, and there were a lot of kids in it playing and talking. Some African kids would be there, too. One day Bridget came up to me and said, "I have this song. It's called 'The Everlasting Rose.'" I looked up and said, "There isn't any such thing as an everlasting rose." She said, "No, it's about my grandmother." And she sang the first part of it, and I realized, "This is very nice." Then, in the bedlam of it all, she wasn't able to write anymore. Sometimes it happens like that. A person gets the first bit, but then they're sort of locked, and even when I encourage them they can't quite finish it. So I came up with the next verse. And then we'd put it down in the recording studio with a guy named Eugene Kelly—terrific musician, lovely guy. It came out really well. A lot of Travellers now are recording. Some of them have been on TV.

How are the Travellers you worked with in the early years doing today?

Some of them are dead—a few from drink, others from traffic accidents. One guy, Tom Keenan, died last year really unexpectedly. We used to call him Brother Keenan. He was a great guy. He just dropped dead, even though he was a great guy for fitness. He played handball and he went to the gym, but he did smoke a lot. Another lad, Johnny McCarthy, was the goalkeeper on the football team. He dropped dead on the pitch refereeing a game. He smoked a lot, too. A lot of them became good family people, but some had their marriages break up. In the beginning [1970s] that was really unusual, but now you have more marriage breakups, just like settled people.

I think the big change in Travelling People is confidence. That's the main thing. Most Travellers now will say what they think, will be quite direct. They feel more fully part of society. In the old days some of the older people would call you "Sir." It was kind of an old-fashioned deference that I never liked because we're all part of the human family.

I've changed a lot since 1974, too. I didn't have much ground under my feet in '74. I didn't really know what I thought about a lot of things. I was brought up a Catholic in the North, in Armagh. And I was beginning to reevaluate the belief system that I learned as a Catholic lad. When a neighbor died who was a Protestant, the rule was that we weren't allowed to go into a Protestant cemetery. So the Catholic neighbors stood outside. I remember thinking,

"There's something wrong with this." Then when I was at university, I was in love with a Protestant girl, and her parents made her pack me in. I remember thinking, "I've got to understand this." Any place you grow up, you take on board all the stuff that's in the air, that your parents do, that society does, and it takes a while to unravel. Some people stay locked up; they don't try to unravel it. But for me it's always been a journey towards understanding, if you know what I mean.

Religion has come up a lot. People mention going to Mass or visiting Lourdes. They've shown us Mass cards for people who've died, and many have religious pictures and statues in their homes and small shrines in their yards. In the 1970s, not many Travellers went to Mass or confession, although they did visit holy wells and curing priests. What's going on today?

I think in the old days when people were living in shelter tents out in the country, maybe their clothes weren't great and there was that social thing about going to Mass—people would be looking at you. There's more confidence today, like I was saying before. But Travellers are also kind of drawn to the miraculous. A couple years ago when stuff was happening at Knock—visions and all—people here were all talking about it.

Headstones are very elaborate now too.

Travellers are quite competitive among each other and always have been. Who's got the best van? Who's got the best trailer? People can be very house-proud. They want all of it to be right, and they'll be saving to buy this and that. When some started buying nice headstones, it became this competitive thing. Then families got together, and the headstones became more and more elaborate. It can be quite a hardship on people, too. If you haven't got the money, you're still expected as a family to put on a good show.

The weddings have become really big, too. In the old days in Ennis, because people often weren't allowed in the hotels, we'd have the reception in the center. They'd come down after the wedding in the church, and we'd have the tables and the food all spread out and do the reception there. It's not fair to Travellers, but it's hard to blame the hotel owners because it's true that places were broken up. I remember one time when our band came up from Ennis to play at the Galway Bay Hotel. We set up our stuff on the wee stage, and there was a table just in front that was set out for us. We sat down and the woman facing us said, "The last band that played here had to lift up their instruments and run." So I was thinking to myself, "Jesus, I have to watch out." What happened in those days, and still happens sometimes, is that the hotel would say dancing must be over at seven. They were afraid there might be trouble. So you'd sit down at three o'clock for a bite to eat, there'd be a few hours dancing,

Elaborate memorial erected by a Travelling family in Drumcliffe Cemetery, Ennis, county Clare, 2011.

and that'd be it. On this particular day, I thought there was no trouble. We came outside and were loading our stuff into my car and the next minute—*bam bam*—a fight breaks out. A lot of hotels are now requiring big deposits for Traveller weddings to cover the damage in case there is trouble.

How do you think Travellers have dealt with all the change?

  I've noticed over the years that certain families have kept the traditional ways. They've kept working the scrap metal, looking for deals, and this and that. And they adapted very well. In terms of the family unit, the young lads would leave school at eleven or twelve and work with their fathers. When I first came to Galway, a lot of the lads had bicycles with little trailers behind them, and they'd be going up and down the hills fetching scrap. I saw that as very positive. I wasn't the kind of person who thought Travellers should stop doing what they did. But, equally, I thought it was good if Travellers knew there were other areas open—other options. One girl I know, Margaret Ward, took a degree in fine art, painted lovely stuff, became an art teacher in Dublin, and married a settled guy. I have a song called "Margaret Knows." The little chorus says, "Margaret knows the fire that glows in the old ways / But Margaret knows that she'll have to find her own way." So it's the sense that it's possible to be an individual but also be strong within the Traveller community.

The integrity of the family unit is still really important to Travellers. If that's loosened or lost, it can have a very bad effect. There's a site on the Bishop's Field [in Galway] where the family units are still very traditional. The lads are out gathering scrap, and their sons are following them. I see them coming back in their vans from far out in the country. That's positive. On the west side of Galway you have Travellers in local authority housing who are not doing scrap, and the fathers are at a bit of a loss. When people have to fill in time, there's more opportunity for drinking.

I also know some fathers who are disillusioned with the idea of education. In some ways, Travellers were encouraged to think that education was a passport to a lot of different things. It is, of course, but the leaving cert [high school diploma] is an abstraction for most. Even mothers and fathers who want education for their kids let them stay home when they don't want to go to school. But more Travellers are going on to secondary, and some like Margaret have gone on to third level. But it's still a small minority. The training centers have provided a net. Some of the kids I taught in Ennis have come back in now as older people to do leaving certificates, especially the women. Some fathers have trained to pass the test to drive mini-buses. Some people are looking ahead and feel that education's for life. That's good.

We've wondered what Travellers thought George and I were doing in the 1970s living in a camp. Do you have any sense of this?

I had done anthropology at Queens University—I did psychology and geography, too. So when you arrived [on a visit to Ennis], I had a warm feeling about anthropology. I remember my first year at university, we did primitive tribes. Then in the second year in one of the lectures, the professor talked about Protestants and Catholics in the North in terms of being tribes. I remember sitting there thinking, "What is this guy talking about? Tribes? What's he on about?" But when he started talking about the banners and the regalia, I realized, "Yeah, we're all tribes." From then on, anthropology was part of me. I appreciated getting that bit of distance to see where I came from. So when you arrived, I was like, "Yeah, anthropologists. Those are real anthropologists." But at the time, you were probably regarded as some sort of exotic species—even being Americans. And to be working with Travellers at that time was to be on the edge.

I remember once, I was in a training program run by Combat Poverty, and there was a group dynamic exercise. We had to be a village, and we had to pick what role each of us would have in that village. I realized I had to be the Traveller—not because I worked with Travellers. No, rather because I was the guy on the outside looking in. I think part of that feeling comes from when I was a kid with TB and I almost died. I was away from home, getting cured for almost two years. Suddenly I was taken away from the mainstream of life and I couldn't really get back, even with my own family. I was never able to talk about it on a deep level until my early twenties, when I was able to bring up some of my experiences with a girlfriend and talk about this part of who I am. I remember a phrase from a book called *The Words to Say It*. It was about a person who had been in therapy and was finding the words to say it. That was big for me.

At Holylands I used to feel that a lot of fighting, especially domestic violence, happened because Travellers couldn't fully express feelings; they didn't have "the words to say it." What do you think?

I remember in Ennis, after a boy and girl from the center would get married, I'd often meet the lassie in town later, and she'd have a black eye. "What happened?" And she'd say, "Oh, I ran into a door" or something. When I realized what was happening, I focused on domestic violence and what it was like when a girl and a boy were just after getting married and he'd hit her. We started to make this book at the center called *Teardrops*. For me it's really important. It hasn't been talked about much, although there have been some courses in Dublin and more stuff has come out in recent years. It needs to be part of programs and education for everybody, settled people as well. Nowadays, of course, some women feel strong enough to get a barring [restraining] order and the husband can't approach her. Even people I know as good people, good guys, can be involved in it because of the physicality of the male. And I suppose part of it *is* because Travellers aren't good at letting their feelings out, their deeper feelings. Even when Travellers have a drinking problem that they *want* to address, they don't do that well in AA groups because they're inhibited about saying, "This is what I'm thinking. This is what I'm feeling."

It's a macho culture, with bare-knuckle fighting and masculine posturing: "I can beat him" or "If he insults me or mine, I'll get him." Very small things can start a fight. I was at a funeral in Ennis, and on the way out of the chapel I heard this woman say to one of her sons, "Are you going to let him call you that?" Something had happened the previous night. And the next minute, the fight started just outside the chapel. In Tuam, a guy stepped over somebody's grave or on top of a grave, and that led to a shooting. Once something happens, it's not forgotten, and it gets brought up again and again.

A Traveller I knew committed suicide. He was a very level-headed guy, a lovely guy and going with a girl. He had been at a party, and at five o'clock the next morning he hanged himself. Then cousins of his, two brothers—first one and then the other—hanged themselves. An important part of the story is that they were having problems with another family in town. This family would attack them in the street. Two weeks ago I was going up to work and met another one of the brothers and his wife. He'd been doing construction and was limping, and I asked him what happened. He said he was walking the dog when a car hit him. Later I met one of the lads who works with Travellers and I said, "Did you hear?" And he said, "Yeah, that was deliberate." Members of this family ran him over! You're talking about trying to kill a guy. Two lads die from suicide and another lad could be killed at any time. That's the extent of the violence now.

Looking back, the 1970s was a real quiet time, especially in a place like Ennis. Hardly anything was happening. A few people had drinking problems, but nothing major. I remember when one of the lads from Ennis went up to Dublin and onto one of the sites. He came back and said, "Y'know, every night someone brings in a car and burns it." "What?" we said. "Burns a car? Why would you burn a car?" We just couldn't believe it. Years later, when I came to Galway, it was happening up at Ballybane. Cars were being stolen and burned. One Patrick's Day I opened the door of the community center, and the next minute there was this *whoosh* and a car just a little bit away went up in flames. I put that into a song:

> *Almost every night a car gets burned out on the site*
> *Almost every day the shades [police] drive in to make us pay*
> *And daddy says nothing at all . . .*

There were young people even then [late 1980s] on the sites in Galway who weren't under their parents' control anymore. The parents couldn't really say, "You're not going out." But in Ennis, by and large, the parents were still in control. Today you'll hear some of the old Travellers saying, "The young ones don't have nature." What they mean is a basic goodness. You have these extreme things happening with Travellers—good and bad. Often the older people look at some of what's happening today, and they just can't believe it. In the old days there'd be a decent fistfight. As the years went on, some guns—shotguns—came into it. Then you had extreme violence happening. People have been badly wounded, even killed. Drugs are now a big thing in the settled community and with some Travellers because there's money to be made. And, of course, extreme violence is the worst possible advertisement for Travellers among settled people who paint them all with the same brush. We're going through difficult times. It's a difficult time for everyone, Travellers included.

9

TUAM

FROM GALWAY CITY WE TRAVELED TO NEARBY TUAM, A TYPICAL MARKET town with an ancient and colorful history. It was first settled in the sixth century when, legend has it, a monk from a nearby religious community was instructed by his abbot to "go, and wherever your chariot wheel breaks, there shall be the site of your new monastery and the place of your resurrection." Jarlath's wheel broke at Tuam. As in other parts of Ireland, religious sites often developed into towns. Tuam grew up around Jarlath's monastery, and the town today has retained a broken chariot wheel as its heraldic symbol. Our interest, of course, was not in Tuam's monastic origins but rather in its history with Travelling People. The town is notable for having a large Traveller population that is uniquely engaged with the settled community.

Although Tuam was just twenty-one miles away, it seemed to take us forever to get to there in a driving rain, and almost as long to find Harmony Hall, the Travellers' community center where activists Mary Moriarty and Martin Ward were waiting in the doorway for us, umbrellas in hand. After introductions to the other Travellers there and biscuits and tea, they gave us a tour of the spacious facility they had been instrumental in creating. It has a homey atmosphere with displays of traditional Traveller material culture—tinsmithing tools, horse tack, and cooking implements—and historical photographs on the walls. Many of the latter were taken by Victor Bewley, the late Quaker philanthropist and driving force behind the settlement movement. While George went off with Martin to find a quiet room in which to do an interview, Mary and I sat down at a large table in the center's library, which

St. Mel's Terrace in Athlone, county Westmeath, photographed in 1972, was one of the earliest housing developments in which Travellers were settled.

had been dedicated to the late Sister Colette Dwyer, the Dublin area nun once responsible for Traveller education.

When we first visited Tuam in 1972, it was gaining a reputation for its success in housing Travellers directly from the road. Today that might not sound like much, but at the time the prevailing view in both government and settlement circles was that Travellers needed to spend a transitional period living on serviced camping sites before they could be expected to adjust to living in houses among the settled community.[1] Our visit to Tuam came about after a prominent Dublin planner and architect, Luan Cuffe, had been invited to present a paper at a United Nations conference on the role of housing in promoting the social integration of minorities. He was interested in Travellers and asked if we would like to collaborate.[2] We agreed and journeyed to Tuam and two other towns (Mullingar and Athlone) to learn more about their experiences. What conditions had led to the housing of Travellers? What difficulties, if any, had families faced adjusting to being housed directly from the road? To what extent had they integrated into the settled community?

One of the earliest experiments in housing Travellers occurred in Athlone, county Westmeath. As a result of a program aimed at eradicating dilapidated dwellings, the town in the 1930s had housed thirty-one Travelling families together in St. Mel's Terrace, a public housing estate. Conflict had erupted between extended families with the result that many moved away. When we visited in 1972, only five Travelling families still lived in St. Mel's. Some had returned to a nomadic life; others had transferred to other public housing in town. On our return in 2011, the terrace itself was gone—demolished to make way for a new development of residences, offices, and commercial premises to be called the "Town Centre Neighborhood." Families, both Travellers and settled people, still living in St. Mel's had been paid to leave, and most were able to buy houses in the town.

In Mullingar, just down the road from Athlone, an enlightened county medical officer named Michael Flynn had helped forty of the town's Travelling families buy homes during the 1950s and 1960s. He achieved this by blocking demolition orders on houses that had been condemned by the local authority but were still structurally sound. With small government grants to renovate substandard dwellings, the new Traveller occupants—now proud first-time home owners—made the necessary repairs and, in some cases, substantial home improvements. One family, for example, moved into an abandoned house, and through hard work, personal savings, and the small grant, they repaired and replastered its crumbling walls, laid new linoleum floors, and hired an electrician to replace its faulty wiring. Over the next few years they added an additional room, painted the exterior, and paved the driveway. Travelling families were dispersed across the town, thereby avoiding ghettoization and the possibility of conflict between rival extended families as had occurred in Athlone. Most of these early housed Travelling families are now well integrated into the settled community.

Tuam had experienced a high rate of out-migration during the same period. As settled people left Ireland to find work, vacancies were created in the town's public housing stock, which the housing authority decided to fill, in part, with seventeen Travelling families. Although it was still relatively early in 1972 to know how things would turn out, there were plenty of positive signs. The families who were housed near one another were relatives; others were dispersed in different neighborhoods and seemed to be adjusting well to settled life. Only four families had been unhappy enough with housing, at the time of our visit, to have returned to the road. The condition of Traveller homes was little different from those of their settled neighbors. Travelling women had discarded their plaits (hair braids) and traditional dress styles like long aprons, shawls, and boots in order to blend in with their neighbors. They enjoyed having running water and the other amenities provided by housing. There was also more mixing between Travellers and non-Travellers; some of the housed Traveller youths had become stalwarts of the local boxing club.

Today, Harmony Hall, the community and education center built by Tuam's Western Traveller and Intercultural Development Association, offers courses and events focusing on cultural heritage, women's empowerment, health care, computer skills, and literacy for Travellers. It also runs social and sports clubs that are popular with non-Travellers and manages the town's community crèche (day care for young children). Nowhere else in Ireland did we learn of this degree of integration; not only do settled people participate in programs run by Travellers, but many also entrust their toddlers to care provided by a Traveller organization.

In 2003 Tuam made headline news as the first town in Ireland to elect a Traveller mayor—forty-five-year-old Martin Ward. Even the *New York Times* covered the story.[3] The article noted that Tuam's new mayor had been born on the side of the road in a Traveller camp and had done much to integrate his people, described by the *Times* as "an ethnic minority of nomads," into Ireland's mainstream. The details of what happened in Tuam, along with broader issues of culture change and identity, are told in the next two chapters—the narratives of Mary Moriarty and Martin Ward.

10

MARY WARDE MORIARTY
Not All Travellers Wanted the Same Thing

Mary Warde Moriarty is outgoing, confident, and articulate. Born on the Irish roadside, the daughter of a tinsmith, she moved to England as a young woman, worked in London, and married an Englishman—a non-Traveller. Since returning to Ireland permanently in the 1970s, she has worked not only to have Traveller voices and perspectives heard but also to help Travellers take control of their future while not forgetting their past. She is also a published author. [1]

I WAS BORN IN A CARAVAN AND GREW UP ON THE ROAD. MY FATHER EDWARD Warde was a very good tinsmith, and so were his brothers—John and Martin. You've John's photo there [pointing]. In the early days my father sold to shops. He'd get orders, maybe a gross—which is a dozen dozen of ten-, five-, and one-quart cans. During the wintertime he'd make all the tins and store them in the caravan. Then when he'd get the orders in spring, all he had to do was put them together. When he got big orders, he brought other people like my uncle John and Ned Fury in to share the work. One would make the five-quart cans, another the ten-quart cans—twelve dozen of each. That way, everyone got a few quid.

I remember the lorry coming out from the shops with the sheets of tin in a big box. My father would measure the sheets with his fingers. Even though he had an education, he still used his hands the way most Travellers did. He made his own compass for marking the tin. All the tinsmiths used to have their own tools. Everything had to be exactly right because if the shopkeeper was selling a quart and it wasn't giving the right measure or if he was selling flour and he wasn't giving the right size scoopful, there'd be trouble.

Tinsmith John Ward at work on the outskirts of Galway City, 1972.

The tin came from England. Then we started getting tin from America or maybe Africa, which wasn't as good. It turned blue, and nobody wanted to buy a blue can because they thought there was something wrong with it. And some would rust fairly quickly. My father made a lot of money during the war because not much trade was coming into the country. He could make something out of anything and sell it. It was tougher in the '50s, and a lot of Travellers started going to England then because there wasn't much work in Ireland. The enamelware was pushing out the tin, and so was aluminum and plastics. A lot of machinery was coming in for the farmers, and that put people out of work too. A lot of Travellers went over to England to work on the buildings [construction]. Some came back but others stayed, and when the old people wanted to come back home, they couldn't because of their children having grown up and married into people over there. A lot of old Travelling People who are still in England would prefer to be back in Ireland.

Looking back, my family wasn't that poor because we had a caravan and a couple of horses and carts and my father rarely drank. He used to take the pledge in January, and he wouldn't drink again until he climbed the Reek [Croagh Patrick pilgrimage], and then he'd have a few drinks with friends.[2] Then he'd be off the drink again to Christmas Day. So that left us a bit more well off. He was a good tradesman and provider. We always had what Travellers called "good value"—meaning we had a caravan, horses, food, clothes, and stuff like that.

When I was a child we were put to bed early—eight o'clock or nine. My father and all the older people would gather around the fire near the caravans. They'd be talking, and sometimes I would be so annoyed because I couldn't sleep. But the funny thing is, years later when people were talking and my father'd say, "I don't know, I can't remember," I'd say, "I know" and then I'd tell them. My mother said, "Mary, how do you know all this?" "I can't sleep at night and I listen to you talk." My father said, "Mary, you've got awfully big ears." Myself and my father always got on, but we fought too because we were much alike. The rest of my family would never open their mouth against my father, but I was always out with it.

My father used to buy the papers on Sunday when we'd all go to Mass. We'd come back and my mother would be making the dinner and any other family that was there would gather round and my father would read the paper aloud. I think half the time he put in things just for the *craic*. In the late '50s he started reading out statements about Travellers and how Dublin was becoming the focus for problems. Later the papers were talking about sites. "What are sites?" we asked him. He'd say, "It's a field with water and toilets and stuff and maybe a fence." The fence kind of frightened them. My grandmother said, "That's terrible. I don't think I'd like that." But he said, "Don't worry about it. It won't happen in our lifetime." He knew how slow things happened.

How did your father learn how to read when most other Travellers couldn't?

He went to school in Galway after he and his brother Jim were taken into care in 1926, through no fault of their parents. My grandparents were accused of taking some stuff, but it turned out that it was a man who stayed with them that did it. They got two months' jail anyway. My grandmother had a baby in her arms, just ten months old, but still she had to go to prison. The police then said they found their children wandering with no one to look after them, but that wasn't true. Families supported each other. If something happened, you knew that some other family would look after yours. Anyway, they caught my father and his brother Jim. The two oldest boys, Pat and John, got away, but my father and Jim were caught and placed in care. My father was eleven and got five years. Jim was nine and got seven years. My grandmother's cousin, Katie Fury, looked after Pat and John for about a week, then another cousin that had no family came up and kept the boys until my grandparents got out of prison two months later. My father always said that when him and his brother Jim were taken into care, the police told lies.

Anyway, that's when my father got some schooling—in care in Galway. When he was old

Children at Avila Park site, county Dublin, 1971. The girl with crossed arms is Catherine Joyce, a prominent Traveller leader and activist today.

A newly constructed rural "site" for Travellers outside Ennis, county Clare, 1972.

enough, he made his way back [to the family], but his brother Jim went to England and later joined the navy. My father went to England for a while too. Then he came back to Ireland and a few years after married my mother and went back on the road. They had nine children altogether, of which six lived. I'm the oldest.

They spent most of their time in Galway and parked for the winter at the edge of Tuam. Travellers only had two seasons: October until March was winter, and the rest of the year was summer, and that's when they liked to travel. My father did any kind of work he got. If the farmers wanted a job, he did it for them. Instead of money, he might get a bundle of hay for the horse or a bag of turf for the fire, or we were allowed to take a few sticks of firewood off the land. If you had that kind of relationship with the farmers, you were doing well.

In 1964 my father bought a little house in Tuam, and we moved in January '65. It was just a little cottage on the same road where he was born. It had a backyard and a front yard but no water. He put that in himself. There were about six families living in houses down Gilmartin Road and just two families on the Dublin Road. After that, more started looking for a place in the town because it was getting too hard to make a living out of the country. My father was friendly with the town commissioner at the time and tried to help others to get houses. They were all extended family to each other.

Mary Moriarty with her father, tinsmith Edward Warde, and young Alan Mongan in 1986. *Courtesy of Mary Moriarty.*

Was Tuam always a place where it was easier for Travellers to settle down?

It was. Travellers used to have a lot of camping places around the town, but then they disappeared. A lot of them were blocked off with stones, which created more problems for the government because that pushed Travellers into public places and neighborhoods. If they had left those old camping places open, they wouldn't have had so many problems. Now there is the trespass law. I can't remember exactly what year it came in. Now if you stay on the roadside, you'll be fined and the council can impound your caravan. It's not good. But the settled population thinks it's a brilliant idea.

How did you start working for Travellers?

I lived in England for a few years and got involved a bit when I came back in 1969, but I was kind of at loggerheads with the local group [ISC]. I didn't like their ownership of Travellers—the way they talked about "our Travellers." Travellers are themselves and have loyalty to themselves. When a Travelling family moved into a house, it didn't mean they were going to stay there forever. But the committee people couldn't understand that. "What's the idea?" they'd say. "We put them in a house." They thought that Travellers would all go into the mainstream and become nice little settled people. A lot of Travellers did move into houses. The women wanted to go in, but the men often didn't, so of course it didn't work. Families moved out, and then they got blacklisted [by settlement committees]. But my thinking was, "They might even settle the next time." And I have been proven right. Sometimes a family settles for two years, leaves, then moves somewhere else and settles for the rest of their lives.

Another thing they couldn't understand was how a family returning from England could show up and expect accommodation. The committee thought they'd already provided enough housing. I'd explain, "They're from here." "Oh no, they're not," they'd say. "This is her son or his daughter," I'd tell them. "They're not on our list," they'd say. Then I'd say, "Where did you get your list?" This still goes on today in some places, which I find very difficult.

To be fair, the thinking was something the same with Travellers. I remember standing in my hallway—this was about 1974. I'd been invited by a social worker to go with her to a meeting in Ennis, and we were getting ready to leave. I had my son with me in his push chair; he was only two years old and I never went anywhere without him because he only came to me and my husband after six years, so he was our treasure. When I opened the door, two of my cousins were standing there. "Do something," they said. They had houses in Galway, but the heat came up through the floor and they wanted fireplaces. "Try to get them to put in a chimney," they said. I thought to myself, "At least you have a house." People were coming and talking to me, but it was always about them, their family. It wasn't about their community, about Travellers. I wanted to help the people living in bad conditions or who were old or sick. This is still a problem. There isn't enough thinking about *all* Travellers.

In 1978 I was picked to go to a big [settlement] meeting in Galway. There were five or six other Travellers there. It was a huge hall filled with people. At the time it would be nothing to get four hundred or five hundred people to attend a meeting, and there were a lot of priests and nuns. You don't see these numbers at all now—that's a big change. This was my first time speaking at a big meeting, and it was intimidating. But I introduced myself anyway. "I am Mary Moriarty," I said. "I lived in England for a long time. I have children and I own a house and I'm married to a settled man." Victor Bewley took the floor then—he was the chair—and people started asking us questions. We [the Travellers attending] were all nearly wetting ourselves. A very good man who worked with Travellers asked me the first question. "How did you meet your husband?" he said—they were all interested in this. "Did he know you were a Traveller?" "Yes," I said. "Well, how did he know?" "He popped his question and I popped mine—'Do you know who I am?'" Then I explained that my husband wasn't a bit surprised because I had a different way of going about things. His family was poor, and he'd known some Travellers where he grew up. He told me he respected me and that he was marrying me and that was it.

That was the first big meeting I ever attended, and speaking gave me confidence, but the kinds of questions they asked us were personal questions. They should have been asking how Travellers saw the future. What did we think of education for our children? What did we think of the living conditions we were in? Should Travellers stay on the road or move into houses or into sites? What should we do? They didn't ask any of those questions because everyone just thought they were doing the right thing. They only wanted to work with people from the Traveller community that would say nothing and agree with everything. Committee people would say things like, "Oh, poor Maggie here and poor John there. They're in a desperate state." And the Travellers were expected to say nothing and just go along.

I worked with Sister Colette Dwyer for years, and I learned a lot from her, but she was a tough woman and arguing with her was a waste of time. There were times when she tried to get me to come around to her way of thinking. I just wouldn't answer. I'd say nothing, and then she knew. "You don't want to do that, Mary." "No, that's not the way it should be." And then she'd say, "OK." She was very well educated, but she always tried to think for other people. This is how Travellers were made dependent. They let settled people think for them and didn't think for themselves. That's why a lot of Travellers later broke away [from the settlement movement] and some didn't want to mix with settled people at all after.

I'm not a great writer because I'm dyslexic, but one of the things I can do is read upside down. I remember this fellow from the Department of the Environment. He was very tall and a bit of a bully. We were in a meeting once, and he said, "No, I never got that [an official notice]. No decision has been made about it." But I knew the decision had been made, so I said, "Excuse me, the letter you were looking at before—that's the decision. It's in that pile." "What letter?" he said. "The one that's under the other one there," I said, pointing. "Come on, shake them out," I said, and I reached over and pulled it out. "I've never seen that letter," he said. "I've never seen that letter. I didn't know this decision was made." He bloody well knew it was made because he was in the room when it was made. Afterwards the local councillor said to me, "How did you know, Mary? How did you know he had that letter?" "I can read upside down better than I can read the other way," I said. They was all very surprised that a Traveller could do that. He [the DOE representative] said to another fellow afterwards, "I was surprised, you know, that coming from that type of background she could read upside down." It was pathetic that a person with education and working for the DOE would do that, and that's the kind of people you have to try to get to do things for you, for your community. It's very frustrating.

In the late '70s politicians were promising us houses, but we weren't getting them. It was wrong. The only way to protest—we'd tried everything else—was to squat. A social worker gave me the idea; she remains nameless because she's still working. We put six families into houses to squat, but it only took two or three days for most of them to be bought off with caravans and boxes of food and stuff like that. Two families stayed, and we ended up going to court, but they were evicted. Victor Bewley helped get us a lot of publicity. But after that the council bought six or eight houses and from then on Tuam started building houses to accommodate Travellers.

In 1980 the government's Traveller Review Body came to Tuam. They invited some Travellers to meet with them, but fortunately we got word of it and a few of us [activist Travellers and supporters] went to the Imperial Hotel for the meeting. A nun stood up and welcomed us in, but I think some of the others nearly wet themselves when we arrived. And when I saw the three or four Travellers that they'd invited—they were all friends [relations] of mine—I knew that they'd been invited just to show the face of the Traveller. When the questions started, my hand was up. The local committee did get a bit friendlier after that. Common sense prevailed. They could see that we weren't going away, that we were going to stick with it to try and help families.

Early on I wasn't allowed into Galway's county council meetings. I was barred. Eventually, myself and Anne Dwyer, may she rest in peace, got into a meeting. Anne was a domestic science teacher and worked with Travellers here most of her life. She was a great woman. When we arrived for the meeting, the assistant manager who looked after housing told Seamus Keating, the county manager, that he wouldn't stand in the same room with "that woman"—meaning me. Seamus said, "Now, John. It is time for bygones to be gone. We have to deal with people, and we have to do our best for the families." So John came in and sat there. He wouldn't even look at me. Eventually we had tea and coffee and it got a bit more friendly. At the end of the meeting Seamus came over and shook hands with me and said that my ideas were good and he'd like to meet again. Then myself and Anne were handed over to John. From then on I worked with John's housing officer Tom Coughlin, who did a fearsome amount of work here, and I had an open door to come in anytime. They listened to our ideas, and a lot of good things happened.

I've been involved nearly forty years, and I still feel like I have to educate people all the time. I feel tired going over the same old ground. You finally bring a councillor to your way of thinking and he is prepared to do something, and then he loses his seat and you get someone new who has no idea. They don't know what to do, or else they do just the opposite of what should be done. With other people, no matter what you say, you're not going to change them, even when they are proved wrong. I could give you names but not on tape. For example, they've housed Travelling families next to each other who they knew would not get on and who they were advised not to put together. But their attitude is, "The family needs to be housed and we have a house. There, that's our job done. We've housed them." Travellers don't want to live next to troublesome families any more than you do. A troublesome family can destroy a neighborhood.

Describe how your ideas about settling Travellers differed from those of most settlement workers?

Well, number one, I knew not all Travellers wanted the same thing. Some people wanted to be more on their own. Others wanted to go into ordinary council housing but not live right next door to other Travellers—they wanted to be scattered a bit. Others wanted houses together.

Number two, we needed different-sized houses. The council used to build three- or four-bedroom houses only, and that meant that Travellers with no children or living on their own got nothing. We had to work with the council to get the idea into their heads that they had to think about everybody.

How much prejudice do you think still exists against Travellers?

There was a situation a few years back in Roscommon where there ended up being more Traveller children in a school than there were settled children. And there was war about it. A local councillor said the Travellers would have to go, that they'd have to move away. I remember going to a meeting and saying, "Wait a minute now. Where will they go?" In the beginning just two Travelling families had lived in the town, but of course all their children grew up and got married, and this is where all the children came from. I asked one of the fellows at the meeting, "Where are you from?" "I'm English," he says. "What are you doing here?" I said. And he said, "I came here and started teaching and I live here now. I'm from here." "Well, you're not," I said, "but they are. They were always from here. They've always had relations in this town. If the town took in two families to settle, then it also took in their children and their grandchildren. It's the same as you coming here from England. Some of your children may leave but some of them may stay, and they'll have a right to live here." An old man who'd always been very anti-Traveller stood up and said, "Mary is absolutely right. The people we are talking about are not strangers. They're from here, and what we have to do is find some way of catering to thirty Travelling children and twenty settled children [in the school]. They're all our children." In the end they brought in extra teachers to help with the children who needed extra help. There's never been a problem.

A young girl practices writing after school at the Spring Lane site, county Cork, 2011.

11

MARTIN WARD

We've Come a Long Way

Martin Ward, fifty years old and the father of seven, was born in a roadside camp and spent his first six years living in a barrel-top wagon before his family was allocated a house in Tuam. In the following narrative he talks about his childhood, his involvement in setting up the first community center for Travellers in Tuam, his election to the town council, and then, in 2003, his becoming Ireland's first Traveller mayor—an achievement so unusual that it caught the attention of the New York Times *and National Public Radio in the United States. He ends with his views on whether or not Travellers should be designated by the Irish government as an "ethnic group."*

I WAS BORN IN GALWAY, BUT MY FAMILY CAME TO TUAM WHEN I WAS ABOUT four. We camped on the Cloonthua Road about a mile from town in a place older Travellers called the sally bushes. Families used to pitch their camps on each side of the road near the little river. My uncles and father used to poke for eels under the bridge there. We were camped there one summer when a car came along the road and ran into our shelter tent. It was lucky no one got killed. After that we moved up the road to a place where cars could see our camp better, and some oak trees gave us shelter. We were there for a year and a half waiting for a council house in Tuam. My family actually originated in Tuam a long way back. Some of my ancestors were evicted from Tirboy [a rural district of Tuam] in 1886. They couldn't pay their rent and were put out and took to the road.

People say you can't remember your early childhood, but I remember it clearly. Well, some of it. We had a barrel-top wagon, a trap, and a big box cart, something like the spring carts that many Travellers used at that time. I remember the campfires at night, a lot of storytelling, and all of the Traveller families that used to come and visit. My grandmother and some uncles and cousins were also living on the road with us. I remember early in the morning hearing the tapping of hammers. It was the men making tin buckets and saucepans to sell in the countryside. The women used to make flowers out of crepe paper. They were a good seller. I remember the children being able to tell when horses were coming by putting their heads down to the road to hear the vibrations of the horses' hooves. Cars were still fairly rare in those days [the 1960s], so you could hear the horses from a long way off.

We left that camp in 1966 and moved into a council house at 48 Gilmartin Road. My father really wanted it because he thought we children needed to go to school. The house was very basic. It had a big open fireplace with a crane for a cooking pot and kettle. There was no furniture, and everyone brought straw upstairs to make beds. There wasn't social welfare then to give you bedding. If you needed something you had to buy it yourself, and we didn't have much money. I remember our first winter when all we had were these old gray army blankets. When we took off our pants at night, the next morning they would be stiff with ice.

I had never lived in a house before, and it was strange at first. But we did have a lot more room, which was good because there were ten of us. We had our front garden where my mother would grow roses and all sort of flowers. She was a keen gardener. At the back of the house my father—God be good to him—planted potatoes, cabbages, onions, and even a strawberry bed. He was a good gardener because as a young man working in the country he learned those skills from farmers. He was a good farrier as well. I'd watch him shoe our horses. He'd pierce and shape the hoof and then burn the hoof by heating the horseshoe in an open fire till red hot. I still remember the burning smell of the horses' hooves. My father used to tell me how to make friends with a nervous dog by feeding him some of the burned horse hooves. Dogs seem to like the taste, and they'd become your friend for life.

The first time I ever saw television was at Owny McDonagh's house—11 Gilmartin Road. His wife was a first cousin of my mother and second cousin of my father. I watched *Godzilla,* the Japanese film—that was about 1966—and I never forgot it.

A couple of years later my uncles Mattie and Bernie and their families joined us at Gilmartin Road. My aunt Biddy lived with her husband Edward and family nearby at St. Patrick's Terrace. There were also some other Travellers around, cousins of my mother and my father. So we had a lot of contact with relatives. There was a great atmosphere on Gilmartin Road.

Living there was my first introduction to the settled community. Apart from the six Travelling families, the rest were all settled people. We had a good relationship with them. I was very friendly with the Kermans—Johnny and Fred and Bosco. People were friendly and helped each other out. During the summer months my father and uncles used to cut their own hay for the horses at the local graveyard, and they used some of the settled neighbors' gardens to store it. My father and other Traveller men used to bring home turf for the neighbors on their horses and carts as some people had no mode of transport themselves. Most Travellers didn't have cars then, so the horses were important. You looked after your horse like you would any member of the family because that was your livelihood. Travellers had great respect for animals in those days.

I remember my first day of school when I was about six. My father took me to the Mercy Convent where my older brother and sister were. The nuns gave each of us a schoolbag, a pencil, and a copybook. I had been there for a week when the following Monday my sister took me to the Presentation School, the other Catholic primary school in town, and enrolled me there. I am not sure why. Maybe she was confused and thought that it was the correct school. My father decided to go ahead and leave me there, and because of this we had half the family going to the Mercy Primary and the other half going to the Presentation Primary. That was kind of unusual.

Education was not important to us kids. To my parents it was only important to be able to read a letter and write our names. That's all that mattered. Everything else was unnecessary and a waste of time. They frowned upon people going off to secondary school because they didn't see any benefit in it. Their thinking was that if you were fifteen, you were too old to be going to school. You should be out making a living for yourself, contributing to the family. People were very poor in those days, and every family member had to contribute. It was all about survival. My father and mother didn't have any understanding about leaving certs [final examinations in secondary school] and all that.

When I left the Presentation School I was barely able to write my name. I hadn't learned much. But then I went to the Christian Brothers School and met Brother Mains. We hear a lot of awful stories about the Christian Brothers today, but this Brother Mains taught me how to read and write. I remember him always saying, "There is no such thing as a stupid child." That was his approach to kids—everybody had the potential to learn. He set goals for us and encouraged us. He gave me comics and small magazines and let me take them home to read. If you came back and showed that you could read them, he would give you a bar of

Martin Ward among the historical photographs displayed in Harmony Hall, Tuam's Traveller center, 2011.

chocolate. He was a fantastic teacher, and I have great respect for him. Even after I left his class, he would check up and see how I was getting on. My parents' attitudes about school also changed. As the years went on, they saw the importance of education and supported my two younger sisters in finishing third level.

I left school at fourteen and found work in a bedding factory in Tuam. It was owned by a Cork man named Dan Buckley. Dan was a great mentor, too. If you did a good job, he gave you praise. If you did a bad job, he gave you a frigging out. He was a great employer of Travellers. He believed in giving Travellers a chance to work, that you could give a Traveller a job to do and that he would complete it. After six years I became a foreman, and I stayed working there for ten years.

Around 1988 I did a youth leaders course and began working for the Tuam Travellers Support Group doing youth work and setting up sporting activities. With Mary Moriarty, Owen Ward, and some other leaders who were really pushing for change and development for Travellers, we set up a youth club in Tuam called St. Christopher's. It's still going strong today. We called it St. Christopher's because he was the patron saint of travelers. We were always looking for activities to involve Travellers in because there was nothing for them in Tuam at the time. We wanted to get them into sports and involved in clubs. We'd arrange soccer tournaments and contacted Pat Galvin in Ennis and Paddy Houlahan in Galway to organize matches.

In the beginning, when we were starting the youth club, we had no facility. There was an old youth hall that wasn't being used, but when Owen Ward, Anne Dwyer, and I approached the committee that oversaw it, they didn't want anything to do with us. They couldn't turn us down flat out, so they put ridiculous conditions on us, like we could only use it between 6:00 and 7:00 PM Well, how can you run a youth club one hour a day? And they said we had to buy our own insurance to use the building.

Fortunately, we had a great advocate on the committee. "Look," he said, "the building is not being used. Just give them a chance. They are trying to better the community. They are trying to keep young people off the streets. That's what I'm looking at, not whether they are Travellers or not. The bottom line is that they're going to keep young people off the streets." It was hard to argue against that kind of logic. So we got to use the hall. We were there six years, and the only damage that occurred was when some settled lads broke in and did some vandalism. Travellers couldn't be blamed because the caretaker was aware of what happened. After six years we were able to move down here into our own facility at Harmony Hall.

We also set up a preschool for Traveller kids [in 1989]. I drove the kids in my own car to and from school for the first year, until we purchased a bus. I didn't make any money because we were paying off the loan for the bus, so I lived on social welfare payments. But it worked out well as the preschool gave our kids an introduction to school before they started primary school. Then, with their ABCs down, they could understand nursery rhymes, name the different colors, and keep up with the settled kids. With the preschool some real education started to happen. When Traveller kids were able to work at the same level as the settled kids, you could see a change in attitudes about education—a real transformation. Over time it led some Traveller kids to go on to secondary school, a few even doing their leaving certs. Today every Traveller child in Tuam at least tries to finish off their juniors cycle [first three years of secondary school].

The mindset of Traveller parents has changed as well. You now hear some parents saying to their teenagers, "Look, you can take your leaving cert; you can go a bit further." That's a new way of thinking. I went back to school myself to do a higher level course in business and youth work, and I got a diploma in community development at NUI [National University of Ireland] Galway. I also got a degree in business and community development through EQUAL Ireland and the Athlone Institute of Technology. It doesn't matter what age you are; you're never too old to learn. There are still Travellers who say, "OK, enough of that. When does this education stuff stop?" or, "What good does it really do us? It's not going to get me employment." I say to them, "You keep up that attitude and you'll never get anywhere."

When it comes to education and employment, Travellers are sometimes the biggest contributors to our own downfall. We can't carry a negative chip on our shoulders thinking that people are against us, that people are always out to keep us down. If we think negative, that negativity gets passed on in our attitudes to other people and potential employers. I firmly believe most settled people are good, decent individuals and that they want to see progress for Travellers. Sure, you always get a few people that have issues with the Traveller community, but overall there's a lot of goodwill. Most people want to see change and progress for others, and it doesn't make any difference whether you're talking about Irish Travellers, Muslims, or Jews.

Can you talk about how you became the mayor of Tuam and what that was like?

As I said before, I got involved in the community in 1988 when we set up St. Christopher's—the youth club. In the early days I got the members of our youth club involved in town cleanups, like in the graveyard and the grotto, and doing community service, like cleaning yards for older people. Then I moved more into the community development side of things. After a few years I was asked to run for the town council. The first Traveller to ever serve on the town council was Ellen Mongan, who was my first cousin. Ellen served from June '94 to May '99. I was elected on the eleventh of June, 1999. I had support not only from Travellers but also from some settled people who thought I would bring some good changes.

I worked hard, but it was only a town council seat, and there's only so much anyone can do. But being a councillor was very rewarding. I developed great friendships with some of the older councillors, like Michael Kelly and Joe Burke. They became mentors. We'd go for a cup of tea every Monday after the council meeting. They taught me how things worked, how to link up and work with people, and how to avoid pissing people off. Joe liked to remind me, "Whatever happens inside council chambers does not come outside. Don't take things personally." That was in reference to my being a Traveller and him knowing that Travellers often take things very personally. He was always saying, "It's not personal; it's politics."

Four years later I was elected mayor of Tuam. I think some people were very surprised. There was a lot of celebration; some people even lit bonfires and all that. I got letters of congratulations from the president of Ireland, Mary Macalese; the mayor of Belfast, Martin Morgan; and many others. There was lots of articles in all the Irish newspapers and even a few paragraphs in the *New York Times*. It was on some radio stations in America as well. One American radio station just rang me up and asked for a five-minute interview. It was amazing that there was so much interest. All the publicity gave Tuam a pretty high profile, and I think it also created a positive image of the Travelling People in town.

While most people were positive, I know there were some who worried about having a Traveller as the first citizen of their town. They wondered if I was going to let them down. But I think I proved them all wrong. The first year I was able to bring some new developments around town. I filled out a wish list of works to improve the area, such as some refurbishment of houses in Tirboy, a new playground, and so on. Today, with the recession, those things don't happen anymore because the money is not there.

Relations between Travellers and settled people seem to be much better in Tuam than in many parts of Ireland. How do you explain that?

It wasn't always like that. When you visited here in the 1970s it was difficult for Travellers to get into places in town. It was difficult to get into pubs, difficult to get into nightclubs, difficult to get into sporting facilities. Changes started happening in the '80s. I think what happened was that our local committee for Travelling People had a vision of finding Travellers jobs and getting them integrated. St. Christopher's, the youth club, was a big step in that direction. But maybe what really broke the camel's back in this town was the election of Travellers to the town council. That opened up doors for us. It showed people that we were serious about making progress, about wanting changes—not just for Travellers but for the overall benefit of Tuam. During my eleven years on the council, we made some great strides. People in town saw that we [Travellers] could make a positive contribution. That being said, you always get some people that want to knock you down—people saying, "What are they getting out of it? Why do they want to get involved?" Sadly, even a few Travellers tried to bring us down, I think because they were jealous of our success.

It takes a long time to build relationships between people, and a single disturbance or conflict can set you back a few years. Fifteen years ago, if something happened in town involving Travellers, every Traveller would be blamed. We would all be tarred with the same brush. I might be minding my own business at home when, say, two Travellers would go up to town and get drunk and break something or start fighting. Well, I'd be blamed just as if I had been there myself. But if two settled lads went up to town and caused the same trouble, nobody would blame all settled people. It was very discriminatory. You can't be responsible for what another Traveller does or for what your neighbor does. People today are starting to understand that, and that realization is starting to break down barriers between Travellers and the wider community.

Years ago Travellers were seen as people that were always receiving, always getting a handout, and not contributing anything. That attitude is changing in Tuam. We are now contributing. In fact, we are the ones who have a community center. We've got our own gym, our own boxing club, and our own youth hall, and we are the biggest child care provider in the town. In fact, we are the only community child care provider. We have places for seventy-two children in our programs, and the majority of the kids are from the settled community. We also provide the premises for the town's youth club. We have a successful music project, which is community based, and we are setting up a community allotment project for Tuam. Settled people are asking us to provide these services, and that's a huge turnabout. Imagine settled people depending on Travellers. This wouldn't have happened a decade ago.

What has been the single biggest change for Travellers in Tuam?

I think it's been in accommodation. When I was a child, it was all tents and caravans, and the conditions were terrible. People were living in camps with no toilets and no running water—no basic sanitation at all. Some wagons were OK, but others were in bad shape. The houses we had on Gilmartin Road were also in pretty bad condition with no insulation and no central heating. In the last fifteen years the council has fixed up some of those houses: added bathrooms, insulated the attics, and put in central heating. They took down some of the old houses and put up modern ones, which are energy efficient. The new council houses, because they have to meet the Department of the Environment's standards, are better than many private homes.

But it hasn't all been good. In the 1990s the last caravans around Tuam moved off the road and into a halting site on the Galway Road. Unfortunately that site wasn't well thought out, and the families were reluctant to move in. It was built so that every two families were expected to share one chalet—a small kitchen and bathroom. I don't know many settled people who would want to share a kitchen and bathroom with another family. The Traveller families said, "If we are going to come in here, we should each have our own chalet." There were negotiations, and the council finally got some related families to go in together. But it didn't work very well. There should have been more consultation when they were designing the site. In Ireland we have a long history of local government thinking they know better and not consulting Travellers.

Today most of Tuam's Traveller families are housed, but it has not worked out well with some of the more traditional families. The council put them into housing estates and simply said, "OK, you're going into this house. These are the regulations." And then they left without checking to see how they were progressing. The families left rubbish all over the place because nobody told him they had to get rubbish bins. No one checked up on them. There were also difficulties between the families themselves. They needed extra help, and admittedly some were not the brightest sparks in the world. There was conflict that was only resolved when some of the families moved away. They went back on the road in the country-side or moved back on a halting site. In some cases the conflict that occurred showed that other Travellers who were settled nearby also wanted their neighborhood to be maintained properly, to be kept clean and quiet.

I remember when my own parents and grandparents were living on the side of the road, there was never an issue with refuse. They disposed of stuff properly. They used the local dump. Sometimes they'd even sweep the road. That's right, sweep the road.

I'll tell you another great change that has come over Travellers in my lifetime. When we were kids, the old Travellers used to believe in the fairy people. They believed in ghosts, and they believed in the banshee [a female spirit, usually seen as an omen of death]. They believed they were real. I knew people who said they saw the banshee and described exactly what she looked like. Some of it was quite scary. That was the culture that we were brought up with. My father and his uncles used a horse nail, like a crucifix, to ward off evil, to ward off the devil. They used to keep horse nails in the collars of their jackets to protect them from the devil. And sometimes they would turn their jackets inside out to keep the fairy people from putting them astray [getting them lost]. I remember hunting one night and the lads were lost. It was a place associated with the fairy people, and two older men turned their jackets inside out and told us, "We won't find our way out of here unless you all turn your jackets inside out." They believed that. But all that has changed with the younger generation. These things are mostly gone—forgotten.

In the old days those beliefs were not just held by Travellers; country people believed them as well. There was a lot in common between Travellers and farmers in those days. It wasn't just all the work that Travellers did for country people. No, you could see the strong connection, the interlinking between them in the beliefs they all shared and in the music and stories they shared. And there was trust. I remember in the '70s when I used to go out in the country with my father, he could go up to a house [farmhouse] and lift the latch on the back door. There was that much trust. I remember one farmer taking up a bucket and saying to me, "Martin, look at this bucket. It's over thirty years of age. The last man to mend this bucket was your grandfather." The grandfather he was talking about had died in 1937.

Those older Travellers like my father and grandfather had a connection with country people that has broken down and been lost. The younger crowd today doesn't have the same respect for the settled community. I think barriers went up after the work Travellers did for country people disappeared and they started moving into town. That's what brought my family to town and started them to settling. They couldn't make much of a living, so they came to town and had to depend on the social welfare. But I had an uncle who wouldn't take the social welfare because he saw it as a handout, and he believed he could lose his family and kids if he took money from the government.

There was a bit of a boom in jobs for Travellers in Tuam for a while [during the Celtic Tiger years]. They started to get jobs, like working in construction. But now with the recession, most are out of work again, and they're back on social welfare. It's not good. People are born to work, to do something, to make some achievement. There's no life in just sitting back and receiving social welfare. It's demeaning, and it's not easy to survive on welfare, either. People that haven't been there say it's very generous, but let them try it and they'll find out. It's tough right now because there are no prospects for employment for anybody in this economy. Lots are emigrating, and it's not just the young, well-educated Irish who are going. Young Travellers are leaving the country, too.

I'll tell you another change. When I was a child and a member of the family died, maybe an uncle or aunt or cousin, your radio and TV was left off for one whole year and no music was allowed in the house. The women would wear black and the men would wear a black patch on their shoulder. Everyone was in mourning for an entire year. Maybe an odd time they'd switch on the radio to hear the news, but that was very rare. It was considered dishonorable to have the radio or television on when you were in mourning. But then people started to question that. Instead of leaving them off for the entire year, it became just six months. After a while, it was down to one month, and today the TV and radio are not switched off at all. That's a major change. But there are some Travellers saying, "Hold on, this is not right. We're not showing respect for the dead."

Many do take the deceased person's clothes outside, sprinkle them with holy water, and set them on fire. They used to do it with the caravans as well. The last one to be burned in Tuam was around 1977. My father objected to it, saying, "Look, sell the caravan and give the money to the St. Vincent de Paul [a charitable society] or give it for a Mass." He thought it was a waste to just burn the caravan. He was also one of the first to say that turning the TV off for an entire year wasn't fair to the children. But he wouldn't agree with what's happened today where people hardly make any sacrifice. A little self-denial and restraint, a little penance, is good for the soul.

Is there any difference between how men and women have changed?

A lot. Women have progressed more than the men. They've become a lot more liberal in their views. Back in the '70s and '80s you had strong Traveller women like Mary Moriarty and Nan Joyce who achieved a high profile. The men always seemed to take a backseat to them. If the women in the family didn't push for something, it wasn't going to happen. I think a lot of the progress is due to women looking after the family and the education side of things.

But it's important to remember that Travellers are a very diverse group of people. There can be an awful difference between the Travellers here in Tuam and those in Dublin. Some Travellers still have very old-fashioned beliefs, including the women, while others have modern beliefs. Some are educated and progressive-minded, and some are more traditional in their thinking. People on the outside think that all Travellers are the same—that we're all at the same level. But it's just not true. I'll give you an example—the short dresses and low-cut tops some Traveller girls wear. It's one of the things that's frowned upon by the settled community. I've had many people say to me, "Why do Travellers allow their daughters to dress like that?" Well, there's a lot of Travellers who don't allow it. I've got daughters and I tell them, "If you want to wear very short clothes, you should be on the beach. Don't go out on the streets dressed like that, or to funerals or weddings dressed like that. Cover yourself up and show respect for yourself." If you don't have respect for yourself, how can you expect others to show respect for you? I'm not old-fashioned. I consider myself very liberal in my views. But like I said, there's a lot of diversity in how Travellers think and act today.

It's the same with education and employment. There are families that say to their kids, "Look, we have to get into the work system. We have to get employment. We have to get an education. That's the way forward. That's how we are going to progress. We have to become part of the community. We can't be marginalized." It's not like the old days when we had lots of contact with farmers. And then there are other parents who don't think this way at all.

Getting involved is easier to do in Tuam, where we've already broken down a lot of barriers. We've come a long way. Years ago we were marginalized. We were just people living on the side of the road, seen as a law unto ourselves. People never asked why we were living on the side of the road or if that's what Travelling People wanted. I remember a time when if you wanted to join a club, they would just ignore you. Now it's no problem with our kids getting into sports or joining other clubs. But there are many towns where Travellers are still ostracized and where there are huge obstacles to them becoming involved in their communities, just like it was here until ten or fifteen years ago.

There is still a lot of discrimination in many parts of the country. I was at a funeral the other day in Manorhamilton, about ninety miles from here. When we arrived, every shop—apart from one supermarket—every pub, and every restaurant was closed. All of them shut down because they were afraid that there was going to be trouble—drinking and fighting. Now this was a simple funeral with only about a hundred people. To me, that is terrible discrimination. It's the sort of thing that used to happen here in Tuam years ago but no longer. When there is a Traveller funeral in town now, every place stays open—every restaurant, every pub, every market. What happened in Manorhamilton is an example of awful stereotyping of Travellers and of people believing in the stereotypes—if Travellers come to town, there is going to be trouble. Well, 99 percent of the time there is never an incident.

How much improvement has there been in how local government in Tuam deals with Travellers?

There is more consultation. It's not brilliant with the housing authority and some other agencies, but it is happening. Before, there was no consultation at all. The authorities would just come out and say we're doing this and that. It didn't matter what you wanted or what really made sense. They were going to do it their way. It's not brilliant yet, but at least they are accepting some advice. Accommodation is one example. The old policy, which caused a lot of problems, was to shovel all the Travellers into one area. They didn't give a damn that they were putting families together that did not get along. You had some very rough families that weren't going to back away from one another having fistfights, and people got seriously hurt. It also brought awful, negative publicity onto the whole Traveller community. If left on their own, these families would never have lived next to one another.

What's happening now in Tuam is that Travellers are spreading out themselves. With the recession and people moving away, we have vacant houses in town. We have about 120 vacant houses, and that has enabled Travellers to be selective about where they live. They are spreading out all over the town, and because of that there's been a lot less conflict between families. There has also been a positive change in the mindset of Travellers about how conflict should be resolved. Some Travellers are now willing to walk away from a disagreement and maybe have a chat about it instead of using their fists. There are still plenty of families who think the other way, but thanks be to God that thinking is beginning to decline.

Now that most Travellers in Tuam are settled, what's happening to their identity as Travelling People?

Over the years there has been a lot of talk among some town councils about Travellers assimilating [into settled society]. They tried it in Athlone when the council housed Travellers in St. Mel's Terrace. And they tried it here in Tuam in the '60s and '70s with families being housed together on Gilmartin Road. Assimilation is not going to happen. Travellers want to be recognized for who they are. It's like the Irish going to Britain. You're still Irish over there, even going back three or four generations. I have cousins that have been in England for four generations, and they still consider themselves Irish and they still call themselves Travellers. It's the same with the Irish in America; they hold on to their identity as Irish. The Irish haven't completely assimilated in America, have they? They may consider themselves Americans, but they still have that family thing for the old country. Well, it's the same with most Travellers. People want to keep their own culture and their own identity.

Sure, some of the lads I knew growing up who moved to England no longer class themselves as Travellers. Some even go under different surnames over there. I understand where they are coming from. They don't want to deal with the discrimination. But I am glad to say that the majority of Travellers are proud of their origins.

I believe you have to be proud of who you are and proud of your parents and grandparents. Many in Tuam are proud, but some young people are also asking questions like, "Why are we called Travellers if we are no longer Travelling? Doesn't being a Traveller mean you

A young Traveller girl clutches her puppy, 2011.

have to travel?" I say, "No, it's just an identity that you have. It means that you come from a certain group in Irish society which is called Travellers."

There is a man up in county Mayo named Tom Sweeney who was involved in the British Gypsy/Irish Traveller Movement in England. Tom goes out to speak to young Travellers and tells them his story. He says, "I was a Traveller once living on the side of the road. I was nomadic. But then I went to England for years and lived in a house. I came back to Ireland and lived in a house. I have children and grandchildren that were raised in a house and have never traveled. And I say, why should they be called Travellers when they have never traveled? Why should they ostracize themselves, put themselves into a box where they won't get the same rights as settled people?" But Tom Sweeney hasn't dropped the word "Traveller" completely. Instead, he calls himself the "descendant of Travelling People." And he's urging young Travellers to do the same. Tom Sweeney is an intelligent man, and every man is entitled to his opinion, but I don't agree with him. I think it's important for young people to keep their identity. My own kids are quite happy being called Travellers. They're quite proud of it. Yes, they sometimes question what it means now that we are no longer traveling, and we have an open debate in our house. I would like my children to keep their identity, but it is for them to decide.

Another thing that's happened with identity is that the Irish Traveller Movement and especially Pavee Point are pushing strongly for Travellers to be recognized as an ethnic minority. I'm totally opposed to that. I think that will ostracize us further from the settled community. They are trying to use the new documentary *Blood of the Travellers* to back up their case that we are a separate group. I was involved in that documentary, and to me it doesn't support their case. Yes, the DNA of Travellers is different from settled people in some ways, but Traveller DNA is very, very Irish. Take my own DNA. The DNA on my father's line relates all the way back to Niall of the Nine Hostages, one of the first kings of Ireland. Now, isn't that very Irish? Traveller DNA is Irish DNA, and it hasn't changed a lot in a thousand years. So how can they argue that we are a separate ethnic group? The current *taoiseach* [prime minister] Enda Kenny had his DNA done and his line is the same as mine.

We are working on a policy paper that would have Travellers recognized as a "native Irish minority," not as a separate ethnic group. This will come from several different Traveller organizations at the national and regional levels that share our view. We think being considered a separate ethnic group would be a disaster. We do not have different ethnicity. To borrow a phrase, what we need is an Irish solution for an Irish problem. I think what would be acceptable to most Travellers is to say that we are a "native Irish minority"—whereas if someone says you're a member of an "ethnic minority," they are really saying you're not Irish, that you're not from this country. Instead of breaking down barriers between us and the settled community, that kind of thinking would create barriers. We need to keep our identity as Irish, not do something that would separate us further from the general population. Some of the people who are pushing the ethnicity idea even want Travellers to have their own flag and their own anthem. That is very, very dangerous and could do a lot of damage to Travellers.

When the ethnicity people talk about Travellers being a separate ethnic group, they never use the word "Irish." They seem to have forgotten that a lot of Traveller traditions and customs are Gaelic Irish traditions, like early marriage and the importance we place on the extended family, our funerals, our wakes, visiting holy wells, how we cope with crises. Even the old Irish clan system can still be found in Traveller culture. If you go back to the Ireland of the 1950s, you will find that the Traveller community and the settled population had the same music. It's hard to distinguish between an Irish singer and a Traveller singer, it's so similar. And so on. I don't know where they're coming from with this separate ethnicity idea.

I also think it's dangerous because it will contribute to the public perception that everything is being done for Travellers, that Travellers are getting this or that free. I tell you that in the long run it will do more damage to Travellers than good. The truth is that you could travel the width and breadth of this country talking to Travellers about this, and you wouldn't find many who have a clue what you're talking about. A lot of Travellers don't know the word "ethnicity." It needs to be explained to the community. Traveller organizations should only push the agenda of the people they are representing, and that's not the case with this ethnicity idea. I am open to change but not at any price.

12

FULL CIRCLE

L EAVING TUAM, WE BEGAN THE FINAL LEG OF OUR JOURNEY BACK TO Dublin with a few stops along the way. In Moate, county Westmeath, we visited Nanny Nevin, who had been one of Holylands' three matriarchs during our fieldwork—the female head of the Maughan "clan." In 1971 she and her husband, Paddy, were recent arrivals to the city, having left Moate after an arsonist set fire to the small house they had just purchased for a few hundred pounds with the help of Michael Flynn, the county's medical officer. At Holylands the couple and fifteen children squeezed into two trailers, with the overflow sleeping wherever they could—one teenage son slept in an abandoned car.

The Maughans were a hard-working family. Nanny, with the help of the older children, fetched water daily from the site's single tap, hand-laundered tub after tub of clothes, groomed the youngest, and prepared food in a seemingly never-ending cycle. Her eldest, disabled daughter Mary, and some of the other girls begged door-to-door in nearby neighborhoods. Meanwhile, Paddy and the older boys collected scrap metal; John, who was nearly deaf, repaired and sold the old bicycles they acquired. Another son worked nearby running errands for a construction company. The family also kept horses, which were valued not only for the work they performed but also for the wealth they represented. When cash was needed an animal could be sold, and mares produced foals, providing healthy interest on Paddy's initial investment.

In the early 1980s Nanny returned to Moate with all but her two oldest sons in order to escape Holylands' drinking and "carry-on," including that of her husband, Paddy. Always

Nanny Nevin Maughan grooms one of her many children at Holylands while daughter Kathleen adjusts her own clothes, 1972.

a teetotaler, she wanted peace and stability for her children and gave Paddy an ultimatum. Before long he followed, and they were eventually allocated a council house much nicer than the one they'd purchased years before. We had many photographs of the Maughans, especially of their gregarious son Anthony, to whom we'd been close. He, along with Michael Donoghue, had accompanied us when we hitched our mare, Franny, to our barrel-top wagon and left Holylands to experience traveling firsthand. Our road trip was an adventure none of us would forget as we blindly navigated our way through the Wicklow countryside, searching for sheltered campsites with adequate water and grazing nearby.

In 2001 George and I had visited Nanny in her new house in Moate. Only the horse heads on the pillars flanking the driveway suggested that the house, on a country road with plenty of space between neighbors, might belong to a Traveller. We had arrived to discover that Nanny's eight-year-old granddaughter had been abducted a few days before. A neighbor had seen a man pull her into his car and reported it to the police. While Nanny's sons mounted a desperate search, Nanny had journeyed to a curing priest in Multyfarnham to solicit prayers for her safe return. The little girl managed to escape when her abductor stopped on the roadside to relieve himself, but the incident was a shock for the family, who now worried about all their young children. When two *gardai* arrived during our visit to update Nanny on the status of the investigation, they eyed us suspiciously, perhaps assuming we were journalists. Even for Nanny, our unexpected arrival after thirty years must have been confusing, although she was happy to see us and misty-eyed when we left. Our current visit with a stack of photographs and a film crew in tow was, in its own way, equally out of the ordinary.

It was a dreary day and raining hard as we hurried to the Maughans' door in 2011. Our knock was answered by Kathleen, Nanny's forty-four-year-old daughter, who greeted us in skintight pants and a glittery tank top that highlighted the Playboy bunny tattoo on her chest. When we'd last seen her, she had been a four-year-old in pigtails and tattered hand-me-downs. Now she was the mother of six. She ushered us into the living room, where Nanny sat in an armchair next to the fireplace, its mantel filled with figurines and memorial cards. At eighty-three, Nanny was still a big woman but no longer as vigorous, and she had lost some of her hearing. She let Kathleen, who had gone to school through third form (about age thirteen), do much of the talking.

Looking at photographs of their family and Holylands brought back many fond memories. Nanny asked if I remembered the griddle bread she used to make over an open fire and the lucky horseshoe she had given me. I did, but I remembered the "pocket" (a type of purse) she had hand-embroidered and covered with buttons and given to me as a going-away present even more. Some images evoked nostalgia and loss. Nanny's son Anthony, our traveling companion, had died of Hodgkin's disease while still in his teens. Her husband, Paddy, had died in the mid-1990s. When George pulled out a photograph of their burned house in Moate and asked Nanny if she knew who had done it, she said she did but declined to name the individual as that person was still around. We'd always assumed the arson, which destroyed much of the upstairs and roof, had been committed by a settled person. While living at Holylands, Paddy had told us that locals had prevented the carpenter he hired from making repairs, but something about Nanny's demeanor and caution (no doubt strengthened by the film crew's presence) suggested that she now thought a Traveller had been responsible. Either was possible, given the vicious feuding that still occurs between some Travelling families and the enmity that still remains toward Travellers within the settled community.[1]

Like other Travellers we'd been talking to, Kathleen and Nanny cited the alarming increase in suicide and the growing problem with drugs as two major changes. Some Travellers act as middlemen for dealers; some are users. Drugs and the gun violence associated with the trade are problems all parents and grandparents worry about. A priest and nun who have worked with Travellers in north Dublin for many years had told me earlier that they believed the drug trade has made Travellers more suspicious and fearful of one another, resulting in less mixing between families and more conflict. "Interfamily feuding is a major problem that hasn't been dealt with by the Traveller organizations," Father Paddy Kelly told me. "I believe this is an even greater problem than discrimination."

Our next stop was Athlone, an ancient town on the River Shannon and the Midlands' main commercial center, where some Travellers had been housed in the 1930s. Here we planned to see Tom Fury and Vincent Jones, whom we'd first met in 1971 when they had been manning an information booth on the work of the Irish Council for Itinerant Settlement at the Royal Dublin Society's annual horse show, a major event in Ireland's summer social calendar. Urbane and articulate, they were among the vanguard of settled people trying to better conditions for Travellers in whatever way they could. Tom was then a customs and excise officer living in Dundalk. He joined its local itinerant settlement committee but also took the county manager's advice to heart—"Tom, do good by stealth"—working

Vincent Jones (left) with poet Cecil Day-Lewis and actor Niall Tóibín at an Itinerant Settlement Week event, c. 1968.

behind the scenes with local officials to find Travellers accommodation. Like some of the other non-Travellers involved in the early settlement movement, Tom had been critical of its paternalism and its focus on assimilation as the solution to the so-called itinerant problem.

At the end of our fieldwork, he encouraged us to write an open letter to all seventy local committees assessing the work of the settlement movement. We somewhat reluctantly agreed. Using some of the same material, we later published an article in an Irish academic journal that concluded that it was crucial that Traveller leadership be developed and that programs for change be based on Travellers' perceptions of what was best. "Ultimately," we wrote, "help must come from within the Traveller community rather than being imposed entirely from the outside."[2] What impact either had is impossible to know, although we heard that some people in the settlement movement had been offended by our letter and objected to criticism from two young Americans. One of the movement leaders, Father Tom Fehily, took the criticism personally and not very kindly, we were told.

Vincent Jones had been a Dublin businessman who returned to Ireland in 1963 after living in England and Nigeria for a decade. "I had just come back," Vincent recalled as we sat in Tom's living room drinking tea:

> It was such a shock to hear about Travelling People living in such dire poverty. On television I saw a family living in a crude tent on the side of the road, and I couldn't believe it. My memory of Travellers was of the Delaneys in my home village, Winegap in Kilkenny. They used to come and mend pots and pans and pick potatoes for a few weeks. The children fitted in well with other children, and my mother, who was a teacher, gave them as much information as she could. She also had them down to the house. They seemed like anybody else, except that they roamed about. I never thought of Travellers as poor. They were just part of the pattern of village life.
>
> When I came back from England as an adult, I was terribly shocked. It just hit me and I thought, "God, I'll have to do something." So I approached Victor Bewley and Father Tom Fehily [ISM leaders] and asked if I could help. . . . At the time, there was a lot of hatred towards Travellers. Every news story was about the trouble they were causing with horses, camping in the city, begging on the streets. I thought there must be a way of improving their situation and humanizing their image.

Vincent enlisted the support of clients in his insurance business. "Listen, I have an idea," he told them. "How about paying an extra pound per month on your insurance policy to help out these poor Travelling People?" Within a few months he had enough money to buy a caravan for a needy family. Over the next few years he bought one caravan after another until he came up with the idea of staging large events—concerts, plays, and readings—to raise money and garner positive publicity. "I got Wesley Burrows, a fine dramatist and the writer of *The Riordans* [a popular and long-running television show],[3] and Cecil Day-Lewis, who was Daniel Day-Lewis's father and a famous poet, to perform in a fund-raiser in the Abbey Theater," he recalled proudly. "We financed quite a lot of caravans that way and created some positive news about Travellers." The following year he came up with the idea of an "Itinerant Settlement Week," a full week of performances, including one by Hungarian pianist Tamás Vásáry, all aimed at helping Travellers. "It only lasted a few years; it took too much to do it right. I know our work did some good, but today whenever I bring up the

Travelling men ask to have their photograph taken at a new group housing scheme in Dublin, 2011.

subject of Travellers with people, it seems to trigger tales of all the people that have been robbed and I have to shut up. If I chat about the old days and the place Travellers had in rural society, I'm promptly put down—'Don't talk to me about them.' And that's a tragedy."

Arriving back in Dublin that night, we took the next day off and drove into the Wicklow Mountains to hike and enjoy the spectacular scenery. On our way back to the city we passed a small housing development barely visible behind a high wall. Sensing that it might have been built for Travellers, we backed up and drove in to find a cluster of six houses and a group of men sitting outside. We got out, explaining we'd once lived with Travellers and had lots of photographs if they were interested in seeing them. While they were looking through them, a young woman recognized her father, Joe Maughan, one of Nanny Nevin's sons. Excited, she immediately rang him on her cell phone and insisted that we see him right then. She'd lead us there in her car.

Joe Maughan and Dickio Connors examine a mare in the fields near Holylands, 1972.

Nell Maughan and two of her daughters reminisce over photographs in their Dublin home, 2011.

As a teen Joe had collected scrap metal with his father and worked part time as a "gofer" at a construction site. Now he owned a fleet of seven buses and a very nice home. As we sat in his comfortable and stylish living room with his wife, Nell, and two of his daughters, photographs spread out on the coffee table and floor, a friend—clearly a settled person—dropped by. Joe did not hesitate to pick up some of the photographs to show him the poverty his family had once lived in, surprising me with his candor. We stayed till dark reminiscing and catching up on what people were doing today, with Nell stopping at one image to tease Joe about the cousin he'd once had a crush on.

With only a few days remaining, we went to see the Donoghues again. John had come up from Galway for our visit, and as we all sat around talking, George asked what people at Holylands had thought we were doing when we lived on the site. "Ordinary settled people believed Travelling People were trash and that we were violent," responded Kevin.

So it was unusual to have people like you living with us. We did appreciate that. We knew you were analyzing us and observing us, but I didn't mind because we were doing the same to you. Everything was different—your way of going on. You had your routine. You'd get up and have breakfast at seven and wouldn't eat again until three. We're the types that eat when we're hungry, not at fixed times. You were both always up in the morning, brushing the teeth. No Travellers brushed their teeth, and some started copying you. We'd take it for granted now—things like that. And we'd never seen popcorn or cereal in a box before, and the Frisbee—the flying saucer. We'd never seen that before, but we were into sport. Then you organized the Wagon Wheels [soccer team]. We beat most of the teams in Dublin at that time. I think most of them were afraid to play us—a load of knackers. They were afraid they'd get the shit kicked out of them.

Kevin had decided to get an education following his family's move into public housing in Ballymun in 1974. "I learned a lot off of you," he told George.

Talking to you, watching your manner—you were the main influence when I seen how educated people could be and how respectful. You'd never barge in. You'd always stand back and then approach when it was right. It was the respect you showed the Travelling People. I was just a spy on the corner watching you guys. You living on the

Sally Donoghue Flanaghan and brother Kevin Donoghue with George in north Dublin, 2011.

Johnny Connors inside his barrel-top wagon at Labre Park, 1971.

site with us was a gift to us and opened up the world. You gave us another perspective. We didn't have to get off the road [back then]. I got off the road for education.

Kevin had later married Trish, a settled girl; all six of their children completed school and have jobs in the settled community, although they still think of themselves as Travellers.

The next day we drove to Labre Park in Ballyfermot, Ireland's first official site for Travellers. In the 1970s it had an open feeling, despite the high-voltage wires overhead and its location in an industrial zone. Since then, the one-room *tigíns* provided to Travelling families have been replaced twice with larger and sturdier houses, but the area surrounding the site has become more built up and the site itself is as crowded today as Spring Lane in Cork, with related families' trailers, lorries, and sheds wedged into every available space.

Of the people we had once known at Labre, only Johnny Connors remains. In 1971 he'd been a cocky teenager living with his grandfather, Old Johnny or "Pudding" Connors. Old Johnny had always been friendly and forthcoming during our early visits to Labre. Now he was gone and his grandson was a widower in his late fifties. Johnny reminded me of some other Travelling men we'd met who, with nothing much to do, seem to have lost interest in life. He had little to say and looked depressed, telling us that he spent most of his days sitting at the kitchen table looking out the window. As we emerged from his house at the end of our visit, a crowd formed around us outside, eager to see our photographs—ones Johnny had barely scanned. The adults engaged in the familiar routine of identifying people and comparing the site today with how it had looked before, one man climbing onto the roof of his trailer to do so. Many asked for copies of the prints, as did the residents of Avila Park, another of Dublin's early sites, which we later visited.

After Labre Park, we went to the offices of Ireland's two most prominent national Traveller organizations: the Irish Traveller Movement (ITM) and Pavee Point. The ITM, working in partnership with settled people, represents and supports more than seventy local Traveller groups, develops position papers aimed at helping Travellers achieve equality, and comments on Traveller issues in the media. At Pavee Point, which conducts research, runs community development and training programs, and works to shape public policy affecting Travellers and the Roma, we arranged to interview its director, Martin Collins. His narrative makes up chapter 13 and describes the strides the Travelling community has made as well as Martin's own journey to social activism.

Like most advocacy organizations, Pavee Point has its critics. While it is credited with successfully raising awareness of Traveller issues and promoting better legislation, it is accused of not representing the views of all Travellers and of being too narrowly associated with a contingent of Dublin families. Its social programs and work to instill pride in Traveller culture are widely acknowledged as positive, but the organization's perceived unwillingness to criticize the antisocial behavior of some Travellers has undermined its credibility with members of the wider public, many of whom regard it as too "political."

Today the big issue both for Traveller organizations and for the Irish government is how Travellers should be defined—namely, are they an ethnic group? Martin Ward in chapter 11 argues that they are not, while Martin Collins in chapter 13 argues forcefully that they are. So far, the Irish government—at least at the time of writing—has resisted calls from Traveller organizations, national groups like the Irish Human Rights Commission, and outside bodies, including Amnesty International and the European Union, to acknowledge Travellers as an ethnic group. The UN Committee on the Elimination of Racial Discrimination has twice criticized the Irish government for its "persistent refusal" to recognize Travellers.[4] Ironically, Irish Travellers in Northern Ireland have been recognized by the government as an ethnic minority since 1997 and in Britain since 2000, resulting in a situation where the same Travelling family wouldn't have to travel very far to lose or gain this status.

One of the people we had yet to visit was Mim Connors, the eldest daughter of Red Mick and Katie Connors, who had been two of our closest friends at Holylands. A pretty and lively twelve-year-old when we had known her, Mim had been responsible for much of the care of her younger brothers and sisters. Now she is in her early fifties and—as we were to learn when we drove down to Gorey, county Wexford, to see her—the mother of sixteen and grandmother to thirty. It was becoming embarrassing to reveal yet again that we had only one child and that he was nearly twenty-nine and not yet married. "There's time enough yet," Mim reassured me. Her life experience in this regard—and that of other Travelling women—was so unlike my own and reminded me of an

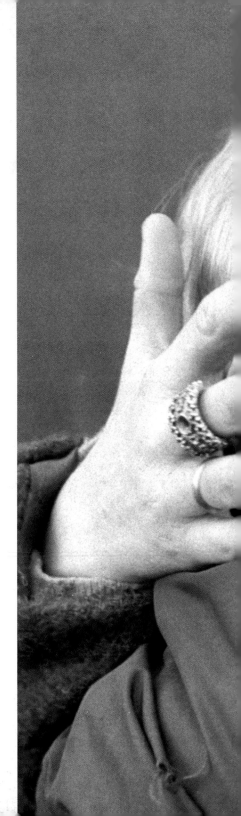

Mim Connors holding her brother Paddy, 1972.

Recent arrivals from the west of Ireland, members of the Mongan family pose in front of their roadside camp in north county Dublin, 1972. Their attire would have clearly marked them as Travelling People.

incident during fieldwork when her mother, Katie, with some of the other Connors women had thrust a baby onto my lap and laughed at my startled reaction. It was clear for all to see that I, unlike their own much younger daughters, had no experience handling babies.

After looking at a number of photographs, Mim stopped to stare at one of her parents. "We never got much sweets or apples or oranges, lads," she said, addressing the half dozen daughters and daughters-in-law who were gathered around. "We'd get a pot of porridge in the morning and a pot of soup in the evening. Whatever was the best they could do, they done it. And they were good to us. They had all the time in the world for us, I must say that." George turned to the young women in the room and asked if they'd rather be living on the road today. "I'd love to be back in that time," Mary replied. "It just seems happier. Better times. No drugs. No violence. It was a better time to rear your children. I'd love to get back to them days." "We had little but it was enough," Mim commented. "Today we have plenty, but it's never enough." It certainly had been a less complicated time, but Traveller lives also had been hard and limiting.

Mim has faced her share of hardships. Besides the deaths of two children, her husband had committed suicide three years before, having been falsely accused of an unspecified act. He was unable to bear the shame. Her father, Red Mick, to whom she was close, had also died prematurely. "Just before he died," Mim told us, "he said to me mother, 'Tell me daughter Mim if anything ever happens to me, I'll be closer to her in death than I ever was in life.'" Remembering this, Mim choked up and paused before managing to utter, "He was a good man." On the way back to Dublin that night I thought about this story and wondered how much Travellers' strong belief in an afterlife eased the decision of so many to take their own lives.

With only two days left before we had to leave Ireland for Tanzania (to set up a new anthropology field program), we made our way to Tallaght for the wedding of Martina Connors, the youngest daughter of Bun Connors and Maggie Moorehouse Connors, whom we had known well in our Holylands days. Back then, Bun and Maggie had lived in nearby Milltown in a rundown trailer and shack on the site of a derelict laundry. Today Maggie lives in a stately house that she bought in rough condition and refurbished with the help of her sons. The contrast could not have been more dramatic, yet signs of Travelling life were still evident. Parked on Maggie's spacious property were two large trailers for additional family members, a camping van, and a small-scale barrel-top wagon.

We were also looking forward to Martina's wedding in part because we had heard so much about how Traveller weddings had changed. Thanks to the British reality television series *My Big Fat Gypsy Wedding,* they had become a public spectacle, and the program had come up frequently in conversations during our journey. Although some younger Travellers may like the show for its glitz and celebrity features, most find it offensive. Peddled as "observational documentary" by its producers, the series paints a cartoonish picture of Irish Traveller culture in England (and that of Roma and English Travellers), using extravagant weddings as a motif. In the words of one critic, it shows Traveller culture as a "debased and ludicrous pastiche of celebrity magazines and soap opera galas," which feeds settled people's prejudices and contributes to public opposition to Gypsy and Traveller site provision.[5]

As Ireland prospered, especially during the Celtic Tiger years, all segments of society became more materialistic and consumerist. "If someone buys an expensive pair of shoes," Bridget Connors told me, "the next Traveller will buy a more expensive pair. If someone buys a ten-thousand-euro trailer, his neighbor will buy a twelve-thousand-euro one." While Travellers' competitive impulses may always have been there, only in the past few have Travellers had the financial means to act on them in a material way, to be "conspicuous consumers." "Children are becoming spoiled," Bridget's husband, Jim, chimed in. "Mine'd be insulted if they only got a Christmas stocking, which I would have been very happy with." Among the many items his children announced they wanted for Christmas were bicycles, cell phones, and a flat screen TV.

Ceremonies like weddings, first communions, and memorial services, where large groups gather, are logical venues for display. Here consumption and competiveness coalesce. "Weddings today are all about one-upmanship," one Travelling women asserted. "I know someone who spent five hundred euros just on balloons." Most of the Traveller homes we visited had framed wedding photographs on the wall showing daughters wearing tiaras and *Gone with the Wind*–style gowns. Stretch limos, Hummers, and Cinderella carriages have also become popular at weddings, as has the erection of elaborate memorial stones at gravesites. Before leaving Ennis, we had visited Drumcliffe Cemetery to see some examples. Carolyn Hou, our research assistant who was following several Irish blogs, had run across threads commenting on this form of Traveller extravagance. "Do you consider it appropriate for social welfare recipients to be spending several thousand on a headstone?" one blogger had written. "The money is not given to people to bling up [create glitzy] graves." Other bloggers agreed until one asked, "Who are they harming? Why do we feel threatened by

The abandoned laundry in Milltown, Dublin, where Maggie Moorehouse and Bun Connors lived in 1971.
The truck and stored scrap metal belonged to Bun, the car to a visiting social worker.

anything that is not the norm in this country? They are expressing their individualism and their culture and we should be open to accepting that."

When we arrived at the Connors home, the family was in the midst of final wedding preparations with Martina and her bridesmaids still in curlers and Maggie in her bathrobe. Despite the chaos, Maggie greeted us warmly and ushered us into her well-appointed living room. No detail had been overlooked. Even the banister leading to the second floor had been decorated with large yellow bows and artificial flowers to celebrate Martina's marriage. Amid the bustle, Maggie and other family members sat down to look at our photographs and remember. Her sister Nan stopped at one poignant image of the Connors men standing outside the church at Jim Connors's wedding in 1971, pointing one by one to all who had died, including her husband Tommy, Bun's son by his first wife. Nan and Tommy had been one of the young couples at Holylands we'd often joined at the pub during our fieldwork. Now, I was touched to learn that she'd named a daughter after me.

Maggie Moorehouse Connors's new home in west Dublin with Cinderella carriage waiting to take daughter Martina to her wedding, 2011.

Upstairs, Martina and other members of the wedding party were getting their makeup done by two young Australians hired for the job. I joined the dressing room drama, helping when I could. Martina had been planning the wedding for over a year, and it showed. Her maid of honor and three bridesmaids were dressed in tastefully elaborate metallic gold dresses. Her own billowing gown and that of her "little bride"—a young niece dressed as a miniature bride—rivaled anything worn by Scarlett O'Hara. Her jewelry and one-of-a-kind shoes would have made Cinderella's stepsisters jealous. As I placed Martina's shoes on the

Connors children participating in the wedding party get ready in Maggie's home, 2011.

Bride Martina Connors receives a momentarily distracting phone call, 2011.

windowsill for a quick photograph, I noticed her mother's goats and chickens wandering around in the yard below and another trailer parked at the back. Although Martina had never personally experienced it, her family's Travelling life wasn't that far behind.

Downstairs, Martina's brother, who would be giving her away, was already in his tuxedo, top hat in hand, waiting for the hired carriage and horses to arrive. The younger boys and

The bride's attention to detail is evident in her custom wedding shoes, 2011.

men in the wedding party were similarly attired, with vests that complemented the brides-maids' dresses. Guests dressed as they pleased, which for the women and girls ranged from subdued suits and pretty prom-night dresses to more revealing outfits, including a black bra and shorts worn by one girl who showed up later at the ceremony. The mood was frenetic yet festive and friendly. As George took photographs to give to Martina and to document how circumstances had changed, Martina's hired videographer and photographer also recorded the event.

One of the most immediately observable changes among Travellers since the 1970s has been in their appearance. Back then, poverty, the weathering effects of living an outdoor life, and social isolation from mainstream Irish society meant that most Travellers had a distinctive look. Today, with housing, access to washing facilities, and more money to spend on clothes and grooming, it is no longer as easy to identify someone as a Traveller by

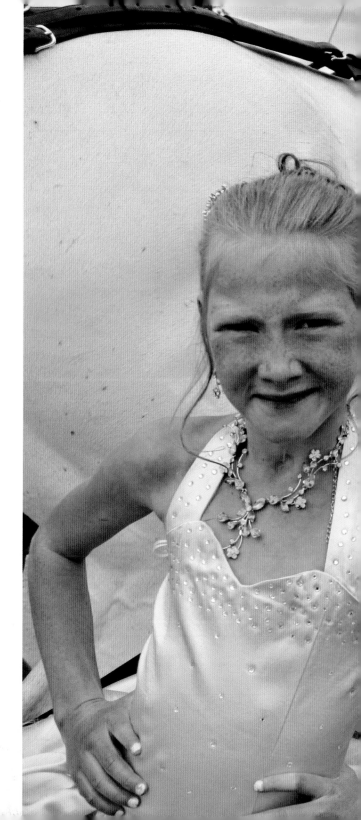

appearance alone. Moreover, younger Travellers are influenced by the same media-driven celebrity culture and styles that influence their peers in mainstream society. Older Travellers are well aware of the change in young women's dress, including what many settled people would regard as "suggestive" attire. Recalling her own youth in contrast, one fifty-year-old woman described the modest dress and careful behavior she had to follow, which included always wearing shoes around men: "My father used to tell me, 'A girl who will show you her feet will show you anything.'" When she got married at eighteen, she'd been to only two movies: a matinee and a film the night before her wedding, which she attended with her future husband and two sisters as chaperones. While most Travelling parents still monitor their daughters' behavior to a large extent, many seem far less concerned about their attire. Many appear to regard even risqué dress as part of being modern and an assertion of individuality, not as an indicator of promiscuity or "bad taste."

At last the fairy tale coach arrived, drawn by two gray horses with two liveried attendants. This would take the bride and immediate wedding party to the church. The rest would follow in stretch limos and private cars. While waiting for Martina, the children clambered in and out of the coach as commuter trains on Tallaght's Red Line whizzed by. The surprised looks on some passengers' faces reminded me of the gawking spectators who had stood at the back of the church at the first Traveller wedding we'd attended years before. Finally Martina emerged and was helped into the coach. As it

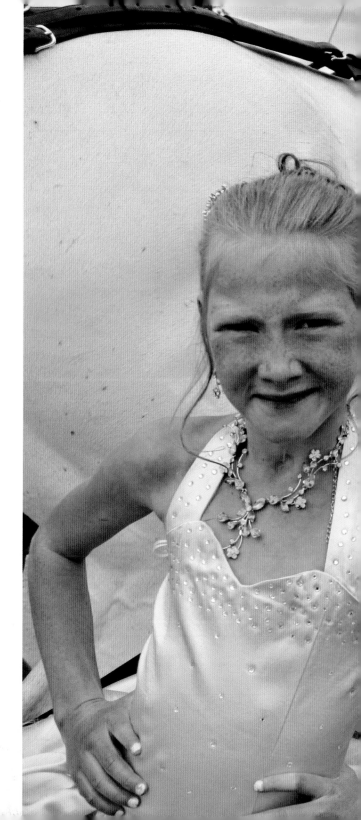

Three of Martina's nieces pose near the wedding carriage, 2011.

pulled away, her brother popped a bottle of champagne. When almost everyone had gone, we got into our own car (as did the film crew) and headed to the church, arriving well before the bride's horse-drawn carriage.

Entering the church, we passed beneath a flower-laden arch to join the other guests. The groom and his best man sat alone in the front pew, appearing nervous and out of place. Slowly those in the wedding party entered. Martina looked lovely, but the unexpected absence of music gave their entry an anticlimactic air. As family and friends shifted in their seats, murmuring among themselves and checking their cell phones, the service got underway. It was a pleasant surprise to have the maid of honor, the bride's sister, rise to read the homily, less so to watch other Travellers slip out for a smoke. Martina and her new husband, Ryan Sardeen, had met eighteen months earlier when one of Martina's workmates introduced them. Soon Martina's planning and hard work would be over and her new life would begin. The next day the couple would depart for a two-week honeymoon in Puerto Rico. While no single event could possibly capture all the changes that have occurred in Travellers' lives over the last forty years, Martina's wedding pointed to some of the more positive ones, such as their greater affluence, confidence, and personal choice. It also brought a singular and sentimental symmetry to our own fieldwork among them.

13

MARTIN COLLINS
Traveller Politics Have Been My Life

Martin Collins grew up in the 1960s and 1970s on a Traveller site in Finglas, on the north side of Dublin. He left school after primary level but a few years later became involved in a training program that changed the direction of his life. Today he is co-director of Pavee Point, a nongovernmental organization whose aim is to ensure Travellers' human rights and to bridge the economic and social inequalities between Travellers and settled Irish society. He is intensely passionate about his work, and he tries to impart to his three children a sense of social justice for all marginalized and excluded groups in Irish society.

MY PARENTS IMMIGRATED TO ENGLAND IN 1965 TO FIND WORK, BUT THEY returned the following year when I was five months old. And after living on the road in Ballyfermot and Cherry Orchard [Dublin suburbs] for a while, they moved into the new Traveller site at Avila Park in Finglas. I've lived in Finglas ever since.

I went to school in Finglas until I was thirteen, like most Travellers did at that time. Not a whole lot has changed in that regard. Then I worked at the dump collecting scrap, and I worked for farmers picking spuds and what have you. Our family traveled every summer doing the fairs and the markets. That's what I did until I was about eighteen, when I met John O'Connell and Ronnie Fay. John had worked in the Philippines for years with really poor people and was trying to organize and politicize them. Meeting him changed my life.

It was December 1984. John and Ronnie came up to Avila Park to tell us about this new leadership and personal development training program they were hoping to organize. We hadn't a notion what they were telling us—it was just going over our heads. But they did generate enough interest and curiosity in us that we went over to their place on Meath Street, in the Liberties [Dublin inner city]. The whole gang of us, all of my cousins and friends all went over.

I'll never forget the first training session. It was really unusual because John, the Lord rest him, had a flip chart and a set of markers and was giving us what I now know to be a social analysis. But at that time, we hadn't a clue. We were just looking at John, trying to make sense of it. Nobody had seen anything like it. Some of the Travellers in our group had been to a senior Traveller training center—a rigid, structured type of training that revolved mostly around woodwork and metalwork skills for the boys, and in another part of the building you had Traveller women doing sewing and knitting and cooking. This was very different. It was kind of a classroom situation where the focus was on leadership, personal development, esteem, confidence building, community development, Traveller identity—a whole range of different areas. Nothing like woodworking.

I remember one of our first classes. We are a group of twenty-four Travellers sitting in a circle, the average age is probably eighteen, and there are both Traveller girls and boys. Anyway, John says, "OK, hands up—how many people in this group have experienced discrimination?" And we all looked at him; our jaws just dropped. John could see the confusion etched in our faces, that we really didn't know the term "discrimination." So then he says, "How many of you here have been followed around in the shop? How many people here have been refused service at a shop?" When he put it in those terms we knew exactly what he meant. It was something we had experienced all of our lives and had to endure almost on a daily basis but had never described it in that way. All of a sudden we'd got a new word to describe our experience—discrimination—and that was really empowering.

Most of us stuck with the program. We met every single day for six months. During it, I became involved in my first protest. It was at a Dunnes Store, kind of a supermarket chain, and the staff was refusing to handle South African products. It was at the height of the Irish antiapartheid movement led by a South African, Kader Asmal, who was living in Dublin. He later became a minister in Nelson Mandela's first government. He only just died. Anyway, they had strikes outside Dunne Stores Shopping Centre, Henry Street, Dublin. So one day John says, "Look, we need to go and offer a little support." He explained South Africa and their apartheid system. That was the first time we had ever heard of apartheid or of institutionalized racism and segregation. Again, all of this was new to us. So we went down there for three or four days, taking turns carrying our banner to give them support. That was an eye-opener for me.

I found out later that when John, Ronnie, and Mervyn Ennis were trying to organize this program for us, they had gone for advice to people who had many years' experience working with Travellers. The advice they got was not encouraging. They were told, for example, that you won't get Traveller men and women sitting in the same kind of learning environment. Well, John and Ronnie did just that in combining males and females in one classroom. They were also told, "You won't get members of different extended families coming together," because Travellers are so obviously tribalistic. And they were told that with everything being based around the extended family, it would be difficult to develop a larger community spirit. But again John and Ronnie showed that the "experts" were wrong. These were very important breakthroughs back in 1985.

Martin Collins talks about his life and the work of Pavee Point, 2011.

At the end of our six months' training, some people decided that it wasn't for them, that they weren't that interested. And they have pursued different things in their lives. One was Thomas McCann, who became the first identified Traveller to go to university. He did a two-year diploma community development course. But others, like Catherine Joyce, who is now the coordinator of Blanchardstown Traveller Support Group, and myself and guy called Michael Collins, who became an actor, continued on with John and Ronnie in a new course on teamwork. In fact, we were given supervisory positions. We each supervised six other Travellers in a new program. Where the previous course was a bit more theoretical and learning-based, this new program was more practical, like on-the-ground lobbying. My work [as a Traveller activist] all progressed from that. It wasn't one dramatic incident or event that led to a sudden awakening—nothing as exciting as that. Rather, it was slow and incremental.

My early experiences in school probably contributed as well. I was actually quite lucky in that my younger brother Michael and me were mainstreamed and not sent to school just with Travellers. As you know, segregated education was the norm at that time. Nobody knew any better. But myself and Michael were sent to St. Kevin Boys National School in Finglas West. There were about two hundred pupils in the school, and we were the only two Travellers.

I started school in 1974 and finished around 1980. I just finished primary; I really wasn't into it. But it was quite interesting because opposite St. Kevin Boys National School, you had St. Joseph's Girls National School, and at the back of that, literally at the back, you had a prefab [building] that was for Travellers only—young boys, girls, and all different ages and different abilities—all thrown in together. It was absolutely so wrong. It was purely containment. It makes me so fucking angry, excuse my language, when I think back on it. It really pisses me off. Those kids in that Traveller-only prefab classroom, like other Travellers in similar classrooms across the island, were treated in the most humiliating and degrading fashion you could possibly think of. They'd come to school, and first off they'd be washed to be made clean and hygienic, just underlining the assumption that you were unhygienic, that you were dirty and smelly. The nuns and the priests and the teachers had to wash you to make you acceptable, to make you "normal."

All my cousins and all of my peers went through that in those Traveller-only classes. It was quite interesting because we all lived at the same site—Avila Park—and we'd all walk to school together in the morning until we got to the junction where myself and brother Michael would enter St. Kevin's school and my cousins and everyone else would enter their Traveller-only school. I will never forget going home in the evening and meeting them back on the site and listening to them talk about what a great time they were having doing arts

Jonathan McCarthy and his non-Traveller girlfriend, 2011.

and crafts, going to swimming pool, playing games, playing football. It was all recreational stuff with very little learning. It was all because the staff, the teachers, didn't have very high expectations of young Travellers.

My father, Lord rest him, didn't give a toss about education. He didn't give a toss. But my mother did. I remember myself and my brother Michael pleading with our mother to take us out of the mainstream class and put us in the Traveller-only class, because we were hearing all these grand stories about such great cracking fun they were having. And they were! But they weren't learning anything.

But my mother absolutely wouldn't have it. At the end of the six years, or whatever it was, at least my brother Michael and myself had learned the basics. We could read and write. All the other Travellers, at the end of their six or seven years, couldn't even read or write their names.

Michael Collins, the guy I mentioned a while ago who was in the training program with me, went to the Traveller-only school. Later he was lucky enough to be acting in an Irish soap called *Glenroe,* but he actually couldn't read the script he was given. He'd bring the script home with him so that his wife, Catherine Joyce, could read it out to him, and he'd memorize it. That's the way he got through the first season of *Glenroe.* He did subsequently go to adult education, and today Michael can read and write better than I can. So quite clearly the ability and the intelligence was always fucking there—again, I'm sorry about the language, but I do get pissed off—but it just wasn't being nurtured. It wasn't being respected.

Why do you think Traveller women in general are more interested in education for their children than the men are?

Ahh, I've been asked that question many times. In the case of my mother, she went for two years to a mainstream school herself in Mullingar, county Westmeath. I suspect that had something to do with it. She wanted her family to get a good start in life. But I also think that Traveller women have always been more interested in education. It was always the women who were the caregivers in the community. It was also the women who traditionally were the liaisons between the community and the state services. The men always seemed to take a backseat, so it was left to the women to liaise with the schools, with the social welfare, with the guards, with whoever. And that's still the reality, although it is beginning to change somewhat.

I also think there's something deep-rooted in Traveller men's psyche that made them think that schools were no use—in fact, that they could be quite damaging to your self-esteem and to your Traveller identity. Maybe they saw schools as a settled person's system and [thought] that it would in some way contaminate us. Not consciously, but perhaps in the subconscious. I think it's something that needs to be looked into, something worth exploring.

What was the thinking behind the decision to educate Traveller kids in separate schools?

It goes back to the '6os. But I haven't seen or read any literature that could tell me why, what it was based on. It seems that if they were thinking about the rehabilitation and assimilation of Travellers, the logical thing would have been to put us in mainstream schools with everyone else. Not in Traveller-only schools. Perhaps it was a case of mainstream schools not wanting Travellers. I think what possibly also happened is that when the Traveller-only classes and Traveller-only schools were there for a while, they took on a life of their own, and you had Travellers gravitating towards them. But at the end of day, they did us a huge disservice and a huge injustice that has been quite damaging to a generation of Travellers. Fortunately, there's a new policy now from the Department of Education that requires Traveller-only classes to be phased out.

What do you think of the work done for Travellers by the early Itinerant Settlement Movement?

Well, the old school has almost disappeared now. The people are no longer active or even alive. The policy back then in the '60s, with the Commission on Itinerancy and the rest, was about rehabilitation and assimilation. That was the analysis that prevailed at the time. There were a couple of big problems with that. One, there was no Traveller voice at the table. It was primarily civil servants and white settled middle-class people thinking that they knew best how the Traveller question should be dealt with. I'm not insinuating that they were bad people. I genuinely believe that they were sincere and they wanted to help what they viewed was an impoverished, underprivileged group of people. So I don't hold any malice against them. I really think they were trying to do the right thing. Actually, I'm glad in one way there were not any Travellers on it [the Commission on Itinerancy] because I think that could be used to lend credibility and legitimacy to the commission's recommendations: "Look, we had Travellers on our committee."

Even if they had actually encouraged Traveller participation on the commission, I don't think there were any Travellers at the time equipped with the confidence, the analysis, and the expertise to engage. I know when I got involved in 1985, it wasn't until ten years later, to be quite honest, that I began to really, really appreciate and understand what was involved in the struggle to effect social and structural change. And during that ten years I had done a lot of training, a lot of personal development, and a lot of leadership training. It wasn't until 1995 that I can honestly say that I fully understood what was taking place. Even then, when I was participating on the Task Force Report of the Traveller Community, I found it extremely difficult—daunting. So I can't imagine that back in 1963, if any Travellers had been invited onto the Commission on Itinerancy, that they would have had any influence. It just wouldn't have happened.

While being on the task force, I saw that settled people and settled people's institutions have a different way of operating. It's just a different dynamic, a different culture, a different way of doing business, of negotiating. It was a different way in which people interact and relate to each other than what I was accustomed to. When you're actually in there for real and you're dealing with maybe twenty-five people, all representing government

Collins and McDonagh children at the Avila Park site in Finglas, county Dublin, 1971.

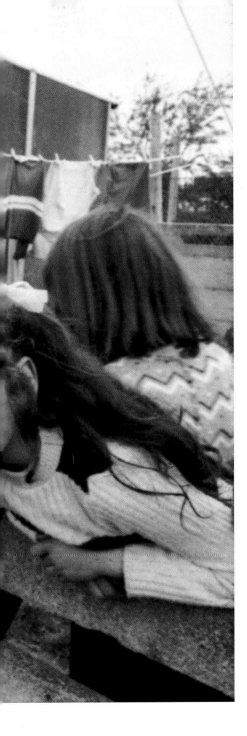

departments—the Department of Health, the Department of the Environment, the Department of Education, the employment agency—and then the politicians, it can be frightening. You have to hold your own, and you also have the pressure of representing your community and not wanting to let it down. You want to get the best deal possible for your community. So, there's a huge load on your shoulders.

Another obstacle is language. I finished school at thirteen, as most Travellers did at that time, and then I was out there picking spuds for the farmers or else collecting scrap iron from the dump. I was not in a position to acquire the same kind of vocabulary as the settled people. Language can be quite empowering once you acquire it, and not having it can be quite exclusionary. You're sitting at a meeting, and all of the people around you have had third-level qualifications and have doctorates and PhDs coming out of their bloody ears, and you left school at thirteen. Even worse, I think sometimes, some people on the task force would use language in a fashion to exclude you, to overwhelm you. So I've always encouraged Travellers as part of their training to acquire the language of the majority population. We need to learn that language, because it is empowering—just like what I described earlier when I first learned the concept of "discrimination."

What are the big changes that you have witnessed among Travellers since you became involved in the Traveller movement?

Well, I'm a political animal, so I'd have to say that the biggest change has been Travellers asserting themselves. That's the biggest and the most positive change from my point of view. We are now asserting ourselves both individually and collectively as a people. We are no longer obedient or compliant or silent.

I think another essential difference today, compared to when you were living with Travellers in the early '70s, is that we are now on a level playing field. Travellers are able to engage settled society more on an equal footing. Today we can influence and shape what gets said and what gets written about us. We were never able to do that in years gone by. We were very passive and very submissive. But things are different now. In fact, we get requests all the time from journalists, from anthropologists, from historians, from linguists, almost anybody you can possibly think of, who want to do a project or research on Travellers. We now have an influence on what's being said about us.

Do you see any change in how Traveller men and women relate to one another?

At one stage Travellers were a male-dominated culture, no doubt about that! But I think there's a transition taking place. It's part of the struggle for equality, for Traveller inclusion. Not just for equality within Irish society but also equality within the Traveller community—between men and women, equality for Travellers who are gay, equality for Travellers who have disabilities. There have been some dramatic changes as people are looking at issues that were once taboo. These are still sensitive areas, but Travellers and Traveller organizations are beginning to look at them. And yes, you see Traveller women asserting themselves today.

Actually, I think many Traveller men are having difficulty adjusting to this new scenario. No matter what community you come from, men basically derive their power from the oppression of women. Sometimes that's how they get their self-esteem, too, by being dominant. That's slowly being dismantled within the Traveller community. There's now more co-decision making, and there are a lot of women involved in Traveller organizations through a bunch of different programs. All of that is giving Traveller women a new perspective. Today it's men who may need to be cared for, to be supported in adjusting to this transition, especially when you consider that there are no employment opportunities for them and all the traditional ways of making a living are gone. I think Traveller men are trying to find themselves. Their traditional role within the community is being challenged. If you look at the suicide rate, you see that for Traveller men it's over seven times higher than for the national population. That might be a manifestation of men needing to find a new way of being.

Why do you think the government should designate Travellers as an ethnic group?

I think people should look at the evidence. Look at the research from different academics—anthropologists—and even constitutional human rights lawyers. When you do that, at least in my view, there's absolutely no doubt that Travellers constitute a distinct ethnic group. We meet all the criteria. The *Mandla* ruling in the UK (1983) took up the definition of what makes an ethnic group, and we meet those criteria. Likewise, we meet the definition contained in the North of Ireland Race Relations Act. And it's the same thing when you look at the different definitions of ethnicity from Australia and New Zealand. It doesn't matter what part of the globe you look at; when you look at all the different research, there's not a shadow of a doubt in my mind that Travellers constitute a distinct ethnic group.

The challenge is how to create an inclusive debate within the community to make sure that as many Travellers as possible are engaged and understand the concept of ethnicity and its implications. At the moment the issue is somewhat elitist, the preserve of a small number of Traveller activists. It needs to be broadened to include other people. But I don't think you're ever going to get a consensus. You're never going to get agreement, and I think the powers that be in [central] government are very disingenuous [in their opposition to giving us ethnic group status]. They are using the lack of consensus among Travellers as a way of not doing anything. They've been using the same mantra for years, "Oh, there's disagreement among the Travellers themselves on it." It's true that we don't all agree. But all of the national Traveller organizations [the National Travellers Women Forum, Pavee Point, the Irish Traveller Movement, and Mincéirs Whiden] do agree and are quite clear that Travellers are an ethnic group. Even CERD [the UN Committee on the Elimination of Racial Discrimination] have twice now recommended that the Irish government recognize Travellers as an ethnic group, as have other human rights bodies. But once again the government gives us their tired old mantra, "Well, the Traveller groups don't agree among themselves."

Sure, there are some dissenting opinions from within the Traveller community. But these are people who don't understand the situation. They believe that the more you claim ethnicity, the more you diminish your Irishness. I say bullshit. They're not mutually exclusive. There is no conflict between nationality and ethnicity. I'm Irish and I'm very proud of that; I am also a Traveller and I'm very proud of that.

The fundamental issue is self-identification. We have the right under international law, in particular, to self-identify. The burden of proof to show that we're *not* an ethnic group is up to the state. And the state has not produced any evidence. All they've said is two things: one, there is disagreement among Travellers, and two, recognizing Traveller ethnicity would have no legal significance. They haven't elaborated on what "no legal significance" means. Again, I say bullshit, there is legal significance and they know it.

On the issue of self-identification I said to other Travellers, "Look, there's a principle here of self-identification. If you don't want to be recognized as being part of an ethnic group, that's your right and it has to be respected. If I and other Travellers want to be recognized as being part of an ethnic group, that's our right." Mutual respect. It's not an imposition. I am not suggesting that every single Traveller must identify as belonging to an ethnic group. They have a right to their own opinion; I just don't agree with them.

One of the criteria of ethnicity is being identified by others as a distinct cultural group. In what ways do you think Travellers differ from settled society?

We do a lot of training with other groups, you know, like guards and schoolteachers on the different dimensions of Traveller culture. We use the iceberg metaphor that focuses first on the observable or tangible aspects of our culture—dress code, language, singing, music, and where and how you live—and secondarily on the large intangible, what is underneath the water, the part people can't see but is there and it's real and it's probably more important than what's above the water, that is, our values and beliefs. We do that as part of our training. But we also make the point that culture is fluid, it changes, it adapts, it evolves—culture is never static—and that we're not stuck in a time warp, that we're not living in barrel-top wagons on the side of the road anymore. Settled people aren't living in thatched cottages and dancing at the crossroads anymore either. Things have changed and are still changing, as you know well.

Going back to your question about culture, I'd say we focus more on ethnicity as a way of belonging, as a way of peoplehood, as opposed to stressing cultural differences. When you frame the debate in that fashion, it allows you to be a member in the group, but it doesn't mean that you would share all the same culture and practices. For example, there are some Travellers who still believe in arranged marriages, and there are some who still believe in early marriages, while there are others who completely disagree with that. You have some Travellers who want to continue a nomadic existence and will fight tooth and nail for that, while others couldn't care less. So there's a whole range of views around some essential cultural practices. The point is that not all Travellers share the same views. But at the same time they want to belong to the Traveller community. So that's how we frame the ethnic debate—it allows you to be a Traveller, but it doesn't mean you have to conform to all the cultural practices.

For example, the other day we were talking about Traveller headstones, tombstones, and how extravagant they have become. They cost a lot of money, like fifty to sixty thousand [euros] each. I know families who are in financial debt as a result; they felt pressured into doing it. Pressured into putting up something that will be on par with what somebody else had done. You shouldn't have to do that, but that's the dynamic right now. My father died last Christmas. He was a very modest man, and he lived a very modest life. Our family got together, and we're putting up a headstone to his memory in the next couple of months. We all agreed on something quite modest, because I don't agree with this new extravagant thing—in fact, I find it oppressive. But shame is a big thing among Travellers. The fear of being shamed can force you to do a lot of things that you don't want to do, all because you are afraid of being looked down on. But no matter, our family is going for a very modest headstone. Modest because that's what my father would have wanted. I know people are gonna talk and try to shame me.

Aren't the lavish headstones the same thing that we see in the lavish weddings, like those portrayed in My Big Fat Gypsy Wedding?

Yes, and I don't like it either. I think the TV show is exploitative. I think it has portrayed Travellers in a really negative way, as being almost uncivilized and barbaric. Traveller groups in England have made a complaint to the broadcasting commission. The Traveller groups there have boycotted the show, thanks be to God for that much. The show is using Travellers who are not politically aware and can't see the implications of it all. Also, I believe that there is some bribery involved, if that's the right word. Channel 4, who makes the shows, has approached Travellers and offered to pay for the wedding cakes and the wedding dress and other bits and pieces if they let the wedding be filmed. Now, I'm not suggesting that there aren't any internal challenges within the community—quite clearly there are, such as bare-knuckle fighting, early marriages, and how we treat LGBT Travellers and Travellers with a disability—but the TV show is way, way off. However, Traveller organizations are responding to these challenges.

They even present men groping young women at weddings. In other words, if you're at a wedding, a nice young Traveller boy of seventeen or eighteen has the right to grab a young Traveller girl and drag her outside. If he gets a kiss off her, then marriage is in the cards. The impression given on TV is that all Traveller families have this tradition of grabbing. Well, I've never heard of it, and no Traveller that I've spoken to in Ireland has either. I mean, I'm forty-five years old and been involved in Traveller politics all my life and gone many times to England for meetings and conferences, so you would think that I would have come across it. But no, I haven't. I think it's simply a case of some Travellers playing to the gallery, playing up to the TV cameras.

There seems to be a lot more violence in the Traveller community today than in the past. What do you make of it?

No doubt about it, it has increased dramatically, with people getting injured, some people even losing their lives, property getting damaged, children's education getting disrupted. We and other Traveller organizations are trying to respond through mediation and conflict resolution and all the rest of it. The biggest challenge is getting Travellers to acquire the skills to engage in dialogue and discussion, to try to negotiate their differences rather than resorting to violence. Among our community there really isn't a tradition of resolving differences and disputes with dialogue and negotiation; it has always been through moving away or bare-knuckle fighting. But now that people are settled in houses, moving away is not practical. Bare-knuckle fighting, as far as I'm concerned, is primitive and barbaric, and it's not a way of resolving disputes. But I do think there are a number of Travellers coming around to the view that dialogue and communication are the way.

If not, this feuding and violence will tear the community apart. The last ten or fifteen years, it's been absolutely unbelievable. Part of the problem is drugs—drug addiction, drug abuse, selling heroin, cocaine, ecstasy, the whole range. It has become a serious problem. You now have Travellers selling drugs for settled gangs, and you have links and alliances developing between Travellers and organized crime. So yes, drugs are part of it.

But there are other issues as well around family loyalties and allegiances, which goes to the point I was making earlier about Travellers being tribalistic. We need to see ourselves as a community rather than as different factions within the community. We need to see ourselves as one integrated, cohesive community, and we're a long way from it. Some of it goes back to our discussion earlier about the role of men and what's expected of Traveller men. That is, a Traveller man is expected to defend the honor of the family, both his immediate family and his extended family, so as not to bring shame. That is the man's role. That is the internal dynamic, which can be very oppressive. We all need to be mature enough to put that on the table and look at it, look at what it means for our community, for our well-being. In lots of cases the Traveller man does not want to engage in violence, but a certain dynamic has been created where he is expected to and doesn't have much choice around it. If he says no, than it's shame and dishonor on him and his family.

I think it's very wrong to suggest that it's just the men who start and perpetuate the violence, because the women sometimes play a very active role by egging their men on: "Oh, you're bringing shame on me! Oh, you're letting the family down!" But overall, what I'm saying is that as a community we have created a dynamic that is strangling us. We've done it ourselves, and I think we're responsible for getting rid of it. There should be no shame on the family to say, "I don't want to fight. I don't want to bare-knuckle fight. Can we talk about this?"

But you know, what's really irritating at times, what really annoys me, is when members of the settled community try to take the high moral ground. "Well, look at the violence among your people. Can't you deal with it?" It's arrogant, as if they have managed to solve the problems in their own community. It's the same with gender inequality. A civil servant said to me recently, "Look, you need to do more to advance gender equality and fairness in your community." Oh yeah, right, tell me something I don't know. But it was said in a way that suggested the settled community is some kind of utopia with gender equality in pay rates and promotion opportunities and all the rest of it. It was kind of condescending bull-shit. Sure, there's a lot we need to do within the Traveller community, but, mate, reflect on your own community. What have you achieved over the last thirty years? You've had laws and policies for gender equality, and you still haven't achieved it, have you? Likewise, with violence and conflict. You are preaching about conflict among Travellers, yet look what's happened in the North of Ireland over the years.

What achievements of Pavee Point are you most proud of?

Probably that the principles and values that we brought to the work back in '85 when we started, which were then criticized and rejected, now prevail right across the country. By that I mean principles of self-determination, Traveller participation, community development, the right to organize as an ethnic group. That they are now widely accepted is an amazing achievement, and it was done at a time when we were quite unpopular. In fact, one of the organizations that funds us received an anonymous letter saying that they shouldn't because we were "radical" and that we were linked to the IRA. I mean, God, can you believe it!

But there're still many challenges around—basic issues like education, accommodation, health care, employment opportunities, and the others we've been talking about. But right now we're struggling to keep the show on the road. We've lost five staff over the last fourteen months. We can't get the money from the government as funding lines have been chopped. Definitely that's one of the biggest challenges facing us. But apart from funding, there's still lots of work to be done around culture, identity, self-esteem, and confidence building. And we need to recruit and educate new Traveller activists if we are going to sustain the movement.

What do you see yourself doing in the future, say in ten years?

I can't see myself doing anything other than this. If I'm not here at Pavee Point involved in Traveller politics, I'll certainly be somewhere else involved in Traveller politics. Traveller politics have been a big part of my life. It has shaped who I am, and likewise, I'd like to think I've shaped Traveller politics to some degree. So it's impossible to see myself doing anything else.

14

UNSETTLED IDENTITY, UNSETTLED LIFE

IN THE FORTY YEARS SINCE WE FIRST LIVED WITH TRAVELLERS, THEIR LIVES have been transformed. The most significant change—and one that cuts to the heart of their identity—has been settlement and the loss of their nomadic life. In Ireland and elsewhere, it is sedentary life that has societal and institutional legitimacy and, therefore, power. It is regarded as the norm, while nomadism is regarded as deviant and in need of control, if not elimination. This is one reason that providing short-stay sites for mobile families has been so strongly resisted over the years: it would facilitate and formally acknowledge nomadism as a legitimate way of life. But the economic underpinnings of Travelling life also have been undermined, which is one important reason many Travellers now seek settlement.

Today the vast majority of Irish Travellers live in houses or in caravans parked more or less permanently on often very crowded Traveller sites. Very few pursue a life "on the road."[1] While settlement has brought amenities, comfort, and new opportunities, it has also left many people, men in particular, feeling lost. Travelling men old enough to have experienced a life on the road miss their horses, the frequent change and daily activities associated with nomadism, the camaraderie of roadside camps, the open air, and the romanticized sense of personal freedom they once possessed. It is also difficult for men to find work, especially in a bad economy. The unique trades and services they once performed are obsolete, and significant barriers to mainstream employment exist due to discrimination and a lack of appropriate training, experience, or will. As a result, many men feel redundant, their despair contributing to a high rate of suicide. In other cultures as well, immobility has placed great strains on once nomadic peoples. Several anthropologist friends who watched *Unsettled,* the documentary about the research journey this book describes, wrote or called to tell us how much the stories Travellers told reminded them of what has happened to the previously nomadic groups they had studied, including the Canadian Inuit and Cree and Aboriginal Australian groups.

Travelling women have fared better than men due in large part to their continued role as their families' primary caregivers and to their greater willingness to engage with mainstream society. They are more appreciative of the amenities of settled life—running water, sanitation, electricity, and appliances—which have made their lives easier. Younger women are having fewer children, creating more time and opportunity for work and community engagement. Women also tend to be more supportive than men of education, both for their children and for themselves.

Gone are the days when Travellers lived on the side of the road, unschooled and illiterate. Now most children attend school until the age of sixteen, when they may legally leave, although only a small minority complete the full six years of secondary school and very few have gone on to third-level education. Travelling youths are considered to be adults much sooner than youths in settled society, which contributes to the disinterest of many in continuing in school. Nevertheless, literacy and education—received not only in school but also in Traveller training centers, work and skills training programs, and specialized courses like those attended by Martin Collins—have broadened Travellers' awareness of the workings of mainstream society and of the wider world and have given them new capabilities. Better educated today, they are also far more aware of their collective history and shared identity with the result that many individuals have a new pride in their heritage. More Travellers now take an interest in and support the work of local and national Traveller-led organizations, which in turn has given the Travelling community a greater voice in public debates about the issues that affect them and in what is said about them. As Aisling Kearns, our research assistant, discovered in her study of the changing media coverage of Travellers, the national media, influenced by organizations like Pavee Point, are far more even-handed in their treatment of Travellers today. Once-common characterizations like "tinker menace," "plague," "nuisance," and "problem" are gone from major publications, although they still show up in personal blogs and the local press.

One of the most important issues being debated at the time of our return was whether or not Travellers make up an *ethnic group*. The difference in opinion, highlighted in the narratives of Martin Collins and Martin Ward, hinges largely on how the concept of ethnicity is defined and on what the implications of applying it to Irish Travellers are believed to be. Opponents, like Ward, say that Travellers are Irish and not sufficiently different from the majority population to be classified as an ethnic minority. "Ethnic," to them, implies having a different national or racial origin. In their view, not only is it incorrect to attribute ethnic status to Travellers but doing so would diminish their Irishness, and this in turn could further damage their relationship with the settled community. Proponents, like Collins, point out that Travellers meet all the accepted definitions of an ethnic group and that legally recognizing them as such will ensure their inclusion in future laws and policies, protecting their rights.[2] Furthermore, they say, Travellers already have a dual identity as Travellers and as Irish; one doesn't rule out the other.

During our early fieldwork we had concluded that Travellers were an ethnic group. One of our first academic publications, "The Emergence of an Ethnic Group: The Irish Travellers," explored how people traveling and living on the side of Ireland's roads for disparate reasons had over time acquired a common identity.[3] In a definition that is still relevant today, anthropologist Raoul Narroll explained that an ethnic group is a population that (1) is largely biologically self-perpetuating, (2) shares fundamental cultural values that are reflected in cultural forms, (3) makes up a separate field of communication and interaction, and (4) has a membership that identifies itself, and is identified by others, as constituting a distinct group.[4] Travellers in the 1970s met these criteria and still do. First, they seldom marry non-Travellers and therefore are largely biologically self-perpetuating, although this is less significant than other factors.[5] Second, although they are culturally very similar to other Irish, they do have unique customs and beliefs, including a separate argot called Gammon or Cant. Third, Travellers interact and communicate primarily with each other. Their main interactions with non-Travellers revolve around economic exchanges and short-lived meetings with representatives of mainstream institutions like teachers, hospital staff, social workers, clergy, and police. And last, Travellers identify themselves as a distinct group known as the "Travelling People," "Travellers," and "Pavees," in contrast to settled people, whom they typically refer to as "buffers" and, in times past, "the quality," "country people," and an assortment of short-lived slang terms.[6] The mainstream population similarly regards

Travellers as different, calling them "tinkers," "itinerants," "Travelling People," and clearly derogatory names like "knackers," "gypos," and "pikeys."[7]

The work of anthropologist Fredrik Barth also influenced our thinking, and it remains especially pertinent to Irish Travellers today. He noted that the cultural differences between ethnic groups can be quite small. What is important is the extent to which group members use ethnic identity to categorize themselves and to differentiate themselves from others. These categorizations, in turn, shape how much and what kind of interaction takes place between groups. Barth stressed that ethnic identity is an *ascribed* status that exists only as long as the social boundaries between groups are maintained. In the 1970s, large segments of the settled population wanted to maintain boundaries between themselves and Travellers. Social distance research conducted in Dublin at the time found that significant majorities rejected the idea of having Travellers as "neighbors" or "family members."[8] More recent studies have found that this is still the case despite the dramatic decline in the most obvious markers of difference between Travellers and the settled community, namely the former's nomadism and illiteracy.[9] Undoubtedly the settled community's negative attitudes toward Travellers today and the belief that they are inherently inferior are bolstered by widely publicized reports of violent feuding, bare-knuckle boxing, sulky racing on public roads, and the serious crime that some Travellers engage in. But ethnic boundaries are also maintained by Travellers who still prefer to rely on each other—especially their extended families—for companionship, friendship, and marriage.

In some areas the boundaries between Travellers and the settled community are being breached. For example, more Travellers today—particularly women—are employed in mainstream jobs. Whether working in shops, hospitals, or community crèches or for county councils or Traveller organizations, their jobs bring them into frequent contact with non-Travellers. Viewed neither as subservient nor as marginal, they fit in well at work and afterward seamlessly return to their extended families and the Travelling community; many live in group housing schemes or on caravan sites for Travellers. We also met independent entrepreneurs who operate businesses not normally associated with Travellers and who deal with non-Traveller customers and clients every day—not as Travellers but as businesspeople. After work, they too return home to their families and the Travelling community. The same is also true of a number of publicly recognized Travellers—sports figures (primarily boxers), popular musicians, singers, actors, and television celebrities.[10] Like code-switching

Anthony Maughan gazes at a new housing development near Holylands in 1972, a portent of the future.

in language, these Travellers are able to modify their mindset and interaction style, when needed, to match the setting they find themselves in and the people they find themselves among.[11] More Travellers are bicultural, that is, they embrace attitudes and behavior characteristic of both communities.[12] The greater confidence and more level playing field created by education, settlement, and the work of Traveller organizations are largely responsible.

Historically, there has always been some "passing" when individual Travellers have chosen to conceal their identity and find ways to merge into settled society. The cases we knew about in the early 1970s often involved individuals moving to England, where the settled community's capacity to "decode" or identify them as Travellers from their speech, dress, or mannerisms was greatly diminished. Once they found conventional employment and moved into flats, they could pass as working-class Irish. A fair number married non-Travellers. Today—with education, settlement, smaller families, and greater affluence—it is now possible for Travellers to accomplish this within Ireland, should they choose to do so. Their primary reason is usually to avoid discrimination—if not for themselves, then for their children. Despite the many positive changes that have occurred for Travellers in the last forty years, they still face discrimination and the disadvantages of ongoing inequality, revealed dramatically in their below-average educational attainment and shortened life spans.

Yet many more Travellers today embrace their identity. In the 1970s most were preoccupied with day-to-day survival and lacked the education and language to think or talk about their collective identity or rights as Travellers. No longer. The emergence of numerous Traveller-run organizations across the country is evidence of this. These organizations do not ask that Travellers be treated better than other Irish people but that they receive the same recognition, respect, and rights that others enjoy. No society can afford to ignore the talent and creativity of any segment of its population. In some places, like Tuam, Travellers are making highly visible and valuable contributions to the life of the wider community through the provision of community day care, sports programs, and other initiatives, including serving in government. With a more level playing field, more Travellers are excelling at a national level and beyond, even representing Ireland in competitions such as the European Song Contest and the Olympics. The rights extended to Travellers thus benefit not only Travellers but potentially everyone in Irish society.

The Travelling community is diverse; its members have different experiences, capabilities, and desires, and not all will choose the same path. As we all know, luck can also play an enormous role in life; some people's ambitions and hard work will be foiled through no fault of their own, while others will stumble into good fortune. The one thing all Travellers have today, however, is much greater choice. The material conditions most Travellers currently live under are abundantly better than they were in the 1970s, and more opportunities are available to them, even in a bad economy and despite continued discrimination. Although greatly changed and no longer as highly visible as they once were when they lived a poor but independent nomadic life, Irish Travellers, as a people and as an identity, are here to stay.

ACKNOWLEDGMENTS

Like most books, this work owes a debt of thanks to many people but foremost to the Connors, Donoghue, and Maughan families of Holylands who befriended and shared their lives with us during our first fieldwork in 1971–72. Living with them was challenging but also a profoundly rewarding experience that changed our perspectives on life. We also wish to thank the many other Irish Travellers living at the Labre Park and Avila Park sites and in temporary camps around Dublin and beyond who helped us.

Many people involved in the Itinerant Settlement Movement also assisted us in both large and small ways. The late Victor Bewley, the driving force behind the movement, and the late Joyce Sholdice, its national coordinator, were particularly generous to us, as were Patricia McCarthy and the late Eithne Russell, both very knowledgeable and caring social workers. We are also grateful to Vincent and Margaret Jones, Tom and Phyllis Fury, David and Moira Smith, Tom and Josephine Murphy, Pat and the late Breege Langan, the late Joel and Betty Barnes, the late Father Michael O'Donohoe, and Cyril White for the cheerful companionship, stimulating conversation, and meals they provided us on many occasions. Their friendship made our fieldwork that much more enjoyable and fruitful. The Joneses and Fureys remain our close friends.

We returned to Ireland several times between 1975 and 1982 and again in 2001, Sharon on a Fulbright sponsored by the anthropology department at National University of Ireland, Maynooth, and George to run an anthropology field school in county Kilkenny. We are grateful to the ten Union College students on that program, all of whom lived with Kilkenny families, for keeping their eyes open and their ears attuned to anything pertaining to Travellers while they attended to their studies. We also wish to thank the following individuals for sharing their insights with us: Liam Keane, Damien Peelo, and Aodh O'Connor, all community development workers with Travellers; Thomas McCann and Grania O'Toole of the Irish Traveller Movement; Father Paddy Kelly and Sister Patricia Lahiff of the Parish of Travelling People; Maugie Francis, National Coordinator for Traveller Education; Rita Behan of Exchange House; Sean Moran, Traveller accommodation officer with the Dublin Corporation; sociologist Anastasia Crickley; and Nolan O'Reilly of Hammond Metal Recycling.

As recounted in the text, the initial idea for the current book emerged in 2001 after Sharon showed our photographs and slides from the 1970s to two groups of Travellers. Their varied reactions made us consider the possibility of returning to Ireland someday and using the images to elicit Travellers' views on how their lives have changed. The opportunity finally presented itself in 2011 and was reinforced by Travellers' enthusiastic responses to a Dublin exhibit of George's photographs arranged by Kieran Swords. A Jesuit Foundation grant from the University of San Francisco supported our return. We were joined by two adventurous and diligent research assistants, Carolyn Hou and Aisling Kearns.

Just a few days into our return, documentary filmmaker Liam McGrath took an interest in our research and asked if he might shadow us with a film crew. Kim Bartley became his co-director. The collaboration created new opportunities for us, and we enjoyed their company immensely—as well as that of cameraman Ross Bartley, soundmen Ronan Cassidy and Colm O'Meara, and Emma Breezing on logistics. The fifty-two-minute film *Unsettled: From Tinker to Traveller,* produced by Scratch Films for RTÉ in 2012, has since aired on Irish television to large audience shares and very positive reviews from Travellers and non-Travellers alike.

We owe a great debt to Ireland's Travelling community, particularly the Connors, Donoghue, and Maughan clans who welcomed us back like family after forty years, even though many individuals in these families were just children when we first knew them. We'd like to take this opportunity to single out and thank the following Travellers for their honesty and contributions to the success of both the film and our research: Dan, Jim, and Teresa Connors; Maggie Moorehouse Connors; Kevin and John Donoghue; Sally Donoghue Flanaghan; Kathleen and Pa Maughan; Nanny Nevin Maughan; Mim Connors O'Brien; Josey Connors O'Leary; and Martina Connors Sardeen. It was deeply moving to see them again, and we were honored by the tribute many paid us when they attended the University College Dublin ceremony marking the donation of George's Traveller photographs to the archive. Thanks are also due to Kieran and Briddie McCarthy, our hosts at the Spring Lane site in Cork, for the opportunity they provided us to live among Travellers again, however briefly.

We are deeply indebted to Martin Collins, Paddy Houlahan, Kathleen Mongan Keenan, Mary Warde Moriarty, and Martin Ward for generously sharing their life stories with us; their personal narratives add immeasurably to this book, and we are very grateful to them.

Others who provided valuable insights into how Ireland and Travellers' lives have changed include Catherine Joyce, Michael Collins, Bridget Carmody, Mervyn Ennis, Pat Galvin, Dermot Hayes, Gerard and Brigeen McDonagh, Mary McDonagh Joyce, Patsy Twomey, Brendan Dempsey, Father Donal Godfrey, Neil Walshe, Adrian Frazier, and Clíodhna Carney. We are grateful to our agent in Ireland, Jonathan Williams, for his support of this project. Thanks are also due to Joanna LaFrancesca and Diane Royal for reading a draft of this book. Rebecca Tolen, our editor at Indiana University Press who has a PhD in anthropology herself, made valuable suggestions and encouraged us toward final revision. This is our third collaboration with Becky, and we look forward to more. We are also grateful to editorial assistant Sarah Jacobi, to Julie Bush for superb copyediting, and to Darja Malcolm-Clarke for safely shepherding the manuscript through the production process.

NOTES

1. FROM TINKERS TO TRAVELLERS

1. According to the 2011 national census, 29,573 Travellers live in the Republic of Ireland—less than 1 percent of its population of 4.58 million. A substantial number of Irish Travellers also live in Northern Ireland and Great Britain, while others live in the United States, the earliest arriving there in the 1800s. Groups like Irish Travellers and the Roma—who originated in India over a thousand years ago and arrived in Europe in the fourteenth century—are usually classified within anthropology as "commercial nomads" to distinguish them from other groups whose subsistence strategies also require nomadism, namely, pastoralists and foragers.

2. John Millington Synge's influential "The Tinker's Wedding" and *In Wicklow, West Kerry, and Connemara*, first published in 1908 and 1912, are notable exceptions. See J. M. Synge, *In Wicklow, West Kerry and Connemara*, essays by George Gmelch and Ann Saddlemeyer (Dublin: O'Brien Press; Totowa, N.J.: Rowman and Littlefield, 1980).

3. Travellers have varied backgrounds. Few people we met in the 1970s knew who their ancestors had been more than four generations back. Many simply said that their ancestors had "been on the road forever," while others, like Bridget Brien Connors, told stories of specific forebears:

> Going back a hundred years or more, me people lived in a cottage in the county Carlow where they was castrating pigs for a living. . . . The old fellow was supposed to be fond of drink. They say he spent all his money on it and got behind in the rent. When they wouldn't let the family in the cottage no more, they had to go on the road. They traveled all of the county Carlow castrating pigs and stopping in old waste houses for the winter. That's probably how they first mixed in with other Travelling People and then the children married into the road.

4. *First Report from His Majesty's Commissioners for inquiring into the Poorer Classes in Ireland with Appendix (A) and Supplement* (University of Southampton: HM Stationery Office, 1835), digitized by EPPI ed., 757, 495.

5. *Tinkers and Travellers: Ireland's Nomads* was published in Ireland by the O'Brien Press and in North America by McGill–Queen's University Press in 1976 and reprinted in 1979.

6. We learned for the first time in 2011 that three people had been named for us.

2. FIRST FIELDWORK

1. The field school, funded by the National Science Foundation, was directed by faculty in the anthropology department of the University of Pittsburgh. That summer its director was Eileen Kane, who later founded the anthropology department at the National University of Ireland, Maynooth (then St. Patrick's College). The previous summer George had participated in the same NSF program in Tlaxcala, Mexico, under the direction of Hugo Nutini and Thomas Shore.

2. See Michael H. Crawford and George Gmelch, "Human Biology of the Irish Tinkers: Demography, Ethnohistory, and Genetics," *Social Biology* 21, no. 4 (1974): 321–31; K. E. North, L. J. Martin, and M. H. Crawford, "The Origins of the Irish Travellers and the Genetic Structure of Ireland," *Annals of Human Biology* 27, no. 5 (2000): 453–65; and John H. Relethford and Michael H. Crawford, "Genetic Drift and the Population History of Irish Travellers," *American Journal of Physical Anthropology* 150, no. 2 (2012): 184–89.

3. We retained a room throughout our research where we had electricity for our electric typewriter, a secure place for our field notes, and a place to clean up.

4. Gammon is a secret argot or cant used by Travellers primarily to conceal meaning from outsiders, especially during business transactions and in the presence of police. Most Gammon utterances are terse and spoken so quickly that a non-Traveller might conclude the words had merely been garbled. The first Gammon vocabulary—known as Shelta in the early literature about it—was published in 1808, indicating that it dates at least to the late 1700s. But some Celtic scholars, including the eminent linguist Kuno Meyer, concluded it was much older.

5. Patricia McCarthy went on to become a social worker with Dublin Travellers and a friend during our research. In a footnote in *Prejudice in Ireland Revisited* (Maynooth: National University of Ireland, 1996), Mícheál MacGréil's study of Irish attitudes toward various groups, the author mentions having spent two months on the roadside with Travellers in 1968–69.

6. The first itinerant settlement committee was organized in Dublin in 1965 by Victor Bewley, a Quaker businessman and philanthropist; Eleanor Butler (also known as Lady Wicklow), a Labour Party politician and architect; and Father Thomas Fehily. Bewley and Fehily remained active for many years, acting as co-chairs of the National Council for Itinerant Settlement. Other important figures in the early Settlement Movement at the national level were Sister Colette Dwyer and Joyce Sholdice.

3. RETURN TO A CHANGING IRELAND

1. They had inherited Byler's disease, a very rare and devastating genetic disorder. See B. Bourke et al., "Byler-like Familial Cholestasis in an Extended Kindred," *Archives of Disease in Childhood* 75, no. 3 (1996): 223–27.

2. Sharon Gmelch, *Nan: The Life of an Irish Travelling Woman* (New York: W. W. Norton, 1986). British edition by Pavanne/Pan Books. Second edition by Waveland Press, 1991.

3. In 2006 the terminology was changed. The Children's Allowance is now called the Child Benefit, and Unemployment Assistance is the Jobseeker's Allowance.

4. *All-Ireland Traveller Health Study: Our Geels,* Technical Report 1 (Dublin: Department of Health, 2010).

5. Mícheál MacGréil, *Prejudice and Tolerance in Ireland* (Dublin: National College of Ireland, 1977), and *Prejudice in Ireland Revisited* (Maynooth: National University of Ireland, 1996).

6. Roland Tormey and Jim Gleeson, "Irish Post-primary Students' Attitudes towards Ethnic Minorities," *Irish Educational Studies,* 2012, http://dx.doi.org/10.1080/0332315.2012.676234.

4. CORK

1. The National Museum of Ireland–Country Life in county Mayo, which we visited soon after its opening in 2001, has a display on the "Tinsmith." By focusing on one occupation, however, it ignores the wider role Travellers played in rural Irish life, including their contributions to folklore and music, and evades the very existence of Travelling People as an ethnic or cultural group.

2. This report was published in 2010 in Dublin by the Department of Health.

3. Mary Rose Walker, *Suicide among the Irish Traveller Community, 2000–2006* (Bray: Wicklow County Council, 2008).

6. THE ROAD TO ENNIS

1. See Adam Higginbotham, "The Irish Clan behind Europe's Rhino-Horn Theft Epidemic," *Bloomberg Businessweek,* January 2, 2014, www.businessweek.com/articles/2014–0102/the-irish-clan-behind-europes-rhino-horn-theft-epidemic; Jim Cusack and Maeve Sheehan, "CAB Seizes Bank Records of Suspects in Artefact Thefts," *Irish Independent,* September 12, 2013 www.independent.ie/irish-news/cab-seizes-bank-records-of-suspects-in-artefact-thefts.

2. "Beor" is the Gammon word for "woman."

7. GALWAY

1. In 1968 residents of Rahoon, a housing estate on the outskirts of Galway City, picketed a proposed Traveller site in their area, forcing the city to abandon work on it. A year later, in a widely publicized incident, a group of residents still angry because several Traveller families remained camped near the abandoned site attacked the families with sticks, uprooting tents and pushing them and their belongings into the street.

2. The Irish Commission to Inquire into Child Abuse released its report in 2009, after a nine-year investigation. It documented "endemic" abuse—beatings, rape, molestation, and humiliation—particularly in church-run industrial schools and reformatories but also in orphanages and hostels between the 1930s and 1990s.

3. Knock, county Mayo, is the site of a major Catholic Marian shrine and a place of pilgrimage. The Virgin Mary, Saint Joseph, and John the Evangelist appeared as an apparition there in 1879.

9. TUAM

1. As one official explained in a December 15, 1969, interview with the *Irish Times,* "The first step towards ultimate integration of itinerants is the provision by local authorities of serviced camping sites. Such sites provide the necessary springboard for the itinerants.... They give local voluntary groups a working area where they can give the itinerants advice and help them map a settled way of life. These sites then act as a bridge ... and help both communities towards a mutual understanding."

2. George later accompanied him to Stockholm to present Ireland's findings. The American representative to the twelve-nation conference turned out to be anthropologist Margaret Mead.

3. The headline of the story, which ran on July 13, 2003, was "Once Scorned, Now Mayor." In 2005 and again in 2010, Pádraig Mac Lochlainn, whose mother was a Traveller, was elected mayor of Buncrana, county Donegal. In 2011 he became the first Traveller TD (Teachta Dála or member of Dáil Éireann, the lower house of the Irish Parliament), representing the constituency of Donegal North-East.

10. MARY WARDE MORIARTY

1. Mary Warde Moriarty, *Turn of the Hand: An Irish Memoir from the Margins* (Newcastle upon Tyne: Cambridge Scholars Publishing, 2009). See also John Heneghan, Mary Warde Moriarty, and Micheál Ó hAodha, eds., *Travellers and the Settled Community: A Shared Future* (Dublin: Liffey Press, 2013).

2. Croagh Patrick, a 2,500-foot mountain in county Mayo, is an important pilgrimage site. Each year on the last Sunday in July, thousands of people climb its scree-covered slopes to reach the place where Saint Patrick is believed to have fasted for forty days in the fifth century and, among other things, expelled snakes from Ireland.

12. FULL CIRCLE

1. For an account of a more recent arson attack on a Traveller home, see "Council's €230k Social Housing Property Destroyed in Fire," www.thejournal.ie/fire-house-ballyshannon-county-council-792065-Feb 2013/.

2. S. B. Gmelch and G. Gmelch, "The Itinerant Settlement Movement: Its Policies and Effects on Irish Travellers," *Studies: An Irish Quarterly Review* 63 (1974): 1–16.

3. The show ran from 1965 to 1979 and broke new ground by being filmed out of the studio on location and by including Travellers as recurring secondary characters.

4. The Committee on the Elimination of Racial Discrimination is a body of independent experts that monitors member states' implementation of the UN Convention on the Elimination of All Forms of Racial Discrimination.

5. Mike Doherty (communications officer at the ITM in Britain), "'Prejudiced' TV Shows Are Turning People against Travellers," July 15, 2013, www.publicserviceeruope.com. The series was discontinued in 2013 after two seasons, although several stand-alone programs were scheduled and an American spin-off series was being developed.

1. According to 2013 figures from the National Traveller Accommodation Consultative Committee, there are 9,911 Travelling families in Ireland, of which 303 (3 percent) live on unauthorized campsites; the remainder live either in caravans on official sites or in houses (the vast majority). Irish Travellers living in England, along with British Gypsies or Roma and other Travellers, are also largely settled, although more remain mobile there than in Ireland, which has done a more complete job of ending nomadism. Some Irish Travellers, based in Ireland and in the UK, travel for periods of time in Europe and beyond for work before returning home to a settled life.

2. Ireland's Equal Status Act (2000) has already singled out the "Traveller community" as a protected group—one that deserves legal safeguards from discrimination. At the time of writing, a key parliamentary committee was finalizing its report on justice and equality, which is likely to call upon the Irish government to formally recognize Travellers as an ethnic group.

3. *Anthropological Quarterly* 49 (1974): 225–38.

4. Raoul Narroll, "On Ethnic Unit Classification," *Current Anthropology* 5, no. 4 (1964): 283–312.

5. Genetic research in the 1970s, while clearly indicating that Travellers were Irish in origin, also discovered that intermarriage over generations had caused them to diverge slightly from the mainstream Irish population at some gene loci.

6. Two slang terms for non-Travellers that were used by Holylanders when we lived in camp were "margarine eaters" and "Storks" (a popular margarine brand), which pointed to Travellers' contrasting (and "superior") habit of eating only butter. At the time of our fieldwork, the Gammon or Cant terms "Pavee" and "Mincéir" for Traveller were not used by any of the Travellers we knew. They became popular later, especially among Traveller activists. They underscore Travellers' unique identity and signal that it is not based strictly on the act of travel.

7. In the past, Travellers were sometimes referred to more benevolently, if condescendingly, as "nature's gentry" and "knights of the road," among other similar terms.

8. Mícheál MacGréil, *Prejudice and Tolerance in Ireland* (Dublin: National College of Ireland, 1977).

9. Mícheál MacGréil, *Prejudice in Ireland Revisited* (Maynooth: National University of Ireland, 1996); Mícheál MacGréil, *Pluralism and Diversity in Ireland* (Dublin: Columba Press, 2011); Roland Tormey and Jim Gleeson, "Irish Post-primary Students' Attitudes towards Ethnic Minorities," *Irish Educational Studies,* 2012, http://dx.doi.org/10.1080/0332315.2012.676234.

10. Although far from complete, the list of accomplished and well-known contemporary Travellers would include professional boxer Willie "Big Bang" Casey and Olympians Francis Barrett and silver medalist John Joe Nevin; singers Shayne Thomas Ward, Chris Doran, Kelly McDonagh Mongan, and Selina O'Leary; actors Michael Collins and John Connors; and television celebrity Paddy Doherty.

11. The term "code-switching" originally arose in linguistics to refer to moving between two languages or between two dialects or registers of the same language in conversation. Now it is also used more broadly to describe the ways people change how they express and present themselves depending on the setting they are in and people they find themselves among. It is often true of minorities and reflects the way ethnicity and culture intersect in people's lives.

12. It could be argued that Travellers are becoming bicultural again. In the past, when the majority of Travellers and non-Travellers were rural and poor and mutually dependent, the two communities—despite real differences—were closer both physically and socially.

peddling, 24, 34
police (*gardai*), 26, 92, 129, 154

scavenging, 94, 150
self-esteem/self-image, 146–47
settlement/housing, 42, 56, 88, 129, 134; adjustment to, 65–66, 71–79, 91, 131, 143; attitudes toward settled Irish, 83, 88–90, 124; history of, 6, 92, 123, 133
sex roles, 146, 186, 194
sites, official, 90, 117, 127, 143. *See also* camps
St. Mel's Terrace, 148
suicide, 68–70, 119, 155, 167, 186, 194

tents, 9–10, 76, 115, 136, 157
tigins, 16, 95, 105, 163
tinsmithing, 2, 51, 73, 107, 125
Tuam, 119, 121–24, 129, 130, 133, 136, 139, 141–44, 146–48, 152, 198

wagons, barrel top, 21, 47, 51, 105, 136, 153–54, 167, 188
welfare/dependency, 22, 46, 53, 74, 145

SHARON BOHN GMELCH

is a professor of anthropology at the University of San Francisco and Roger Thayer Stone Professor of Anthropology at Union College. She is the author of eight books, including *Nan: The Life of an Irish Travelling Woman*; *Tinkers and Travellers: Ireland's Nomads*; *The Tlingit Encounter with Photography*; and, with G. Gmelch, *Tasting the Good Life: Wine Tourism in the Napa Valley*.

GEORGE GMELCH

is a professor of anthropology at the University of San Francisco and Union College. He is the author or co-author of a dozen books, including *The Irish Tinkers: The Urbanization of an Itinerant People*; *Behind the Smile: The Working Lives of Caribbean Tourism*; and, with S. B. Gmelch, *Tasting the Good Life: Wine Tourism in the Napa Valley*.

EDITOR Rebecca Tolen

ASSISTANT EDITOR Sarah Jacobi

PROJECT MANAGER Darja Malcolm-Clarke

MARKETING DIRECTOR Dave Hulsey

EDITORIAL AND PRODUCTION DIRECTOR Bernadette Zoss

BOOK AND COVER DESIGNER Jennifer L. Witzke

PRINTER Four Colour Imports